S0-BCG-691

A Nation of Millionaires

A Nation of Millionaires

Unleashing America's Economic Potential

Robert J. Genetski

THE HEARTLAND INSTITUTE
Palatine, Illinois

Copyright © 1997 by Robert J. Genetski

All rights reserved.
No part of this book may be reproduced in any form
or by any electronic or mechanical means, including
information storage and retrieval systems, without written
permission from the publisher, except by a reviewer who
may quote passages in a review.

Published by The Heartland Institute
800 East Northwest Highway #1080
Palatine, Illinois 60067

Library of Congress Cataloging-in-Publication Data

Genetski, Robert J.
   A nation of millionaires : unleashing America's economic potential
/ Robert J. Genetski.
      p.   cm.
   Includes bibliographical references (p.   ) and index.
   ISBN 1–56833–094–4 (cloth : alk. paper). — ISBN 0–9632027–4–X
(pbk. : alk. paper)
      1. United States—Economic policy—1993– 2. United States
—Economic conditions—1981– 3. Free enterprise—United States.
4. Millionaires—United States. I. Title.
   HC106.82.G46   1997
   330.973—dc21   96-53426
                                                              CIP

ISBN 0–9632027–4–X (pbk. : alk. paper)

Distributed by National Book Network

♾™ The paper used in this publication meets the minimum requirements of
American National Standard for Information Sciences—Permanence of
Paper for Printed Library Materials, ANSI Z39.48–1984.
Manufactured in the United States of America.

CONTENTS

Part Two: Long-Term Planning

Part Three: Cutting the Cost of Government

FOREWORD

Only four days before the 1996 elections, Congressman Mark Sanford (R-S.C.) invited me to discuss Social Security privatization at a town hall meeting in his district. While the nearly 150 people in the audience had many questions and concerns, they clearly recognized the looming crisis facing the U.S. Social Security system and were enthusiastic about the opportunities that privatization offered. On Election Day, Representative Sanford was reelected with 96 percent of the vote. He had no opposition from the Democratic Party.

While Sanford's landslide certainly cannot be interpreted as representing a mandate for privatizing Social Security, his willingness to address, at that moment, such a difficult issue reflects the tremendous change that is occurring in the U.S. political landscape. Former House Speaker Tip O'Neill called Social Security the "third rail" of American politics—touch it and your political career dies. That was because of a perception that American voters would not tolerate any major changes to the program.

But Americans are increasingly willing to face up to the need to reform Social Security and other entitlement programs. Recent polls by organizations as diverse as the Cato Institute and the Employee Benefits Research Institute (EBRI) have shown solid majorities of the American public support transforming Social Security from a bankrupt pay-as-you-go, "defined benefit" program to a system based on individually owned, privately invested accounts. Politicians from both major parties have been speaking out more often on this critical issue. Clearly, Social Security is no longer the third rail.

That Americans are willing to reform Social Security is surely a hopeful sign of their desire to reform other programs of the welfare state. The two major political parties have acknowledged the need to reform the Medicare system. And, last year, Congress repealed the federal entitlement to welfare—the first repeal of an entitlement program in 60 years.

In this book, Robert Genetski has laid out an ambitious program for reforming the welfare state in America, tackling issues from health care to the environment, from education to Social Security. His concise, market-oriented agenda could transform U.S. society and lead to an extraordinary burst of economic growth and prosperity.

I have seen firsthand what such an agenda can do. When I was asked 17 years ago to become Minister of Labor and Social Security in Chile, our retirement system was in shambles. Rather than the usual short-term fixes of raising taxes or cutting benefits, we decided to take the bull by the horns. The result was a privately administered, national system of Pension Savings Accounts (PSAs) that is completely replacing our government-run, pay-as-you-go social security system.

After almost 16 years of operation, Chile's reform has proven itself. Pensions in the new private system already are 50 percent to 100 percent higher than they were in the state-run system. The resources administered by the private pension funds amount to 40 percent of GNP. By improving the functioning of both the capital and the labor markets, pension privatization has been one of the key reforms that has pushed the growth rate of the economy upward, from its historical 3 percent a year to 7 percent on average during the last 10 years. The Chilean savings rate has increased to 27 percent of GNP, and the unemployment rate has fallen to 5 percent since the reform was undertaken.

In the United States, Social Security privatization could have a similar impact. Privatization can prevent the system from going bankrupt, without devastating increases in the payroll tax or cuts in benefits. At the same time, privatization would increase the benefits for future retirees, providing them with a far higher return on their investment.

Privatizing Social Security will also create a nation of savers, spurring economic growth and prosperity. Indeed, Harvard professor Martin Feldstein estimates that "the combination of the improved labor market incentives and the higher real return on savings [from moving to a fully funded Social Security system] has a net present value gain of more than $15 trillion, an amount equivalent to 3 percent of each future year's GDP forever."

But perhaps most important, as Genetski points out, such a change "will strengthen traditional values and promote true freedom and responsibility among the greatest number of people." In other words, privatization will strengthen civil society.

While privatizing Social Security alone would be one of the most important reforms ever undertaken in this country, Genetski's agenda goes even further. In this book he demonstrates how medical savings accounts can reduce health care costs while guaranteeing patient choice, and how cutting taxes and regulation can lead to more jobs and increased wages.

On education, Genetski calls for an end to the government's monopoly over elementary and secondary education, 88 percent of which is provided or controlled by the public sector. He sees school choice and the use of vouchers as the solution to the crisis in the education system. Writes Genetski: "The combination of incentives and competitive pressures would force education to be as efficient as other private businesses. Inefficient schools that failed to produce a high-quality product would lose students. . . . Efficient schools producing a high-quality education would prosper." And so would students, especially those from the inner city, where the public education system has failed to deliver even the most basic skills.

I have seen a country transformed from socialism to free markets. I know firsthand that only free markets and individual liberty can build prosperity for every citizen. If American political leaders were to follow the advice in this book, they would build the best possible bridge to the 21st century, a bridge whose solid foundations would be those permanent American values of self reliance and individual responsibility.

José Piñera
November 1996

ACKNOWLEDGMENTS

The main idea in this book is that each individual possesses the talent to create enormous wealth. Neither this idea nor any of the specific wealth-creating recommendations presented here is original. The great economic philosophers, both past and present, have contributed to our understanding of the importance of economic freedom and the role of the individual in creating wealth. It is to them that this book is dedicated.

The single greatest contribution to understanding these forces came from the eighteenth-century Scottish economist, Adam Smith. Smith's insights might long since have been considered obsolete if not for the contributions of Friedrich Hayek and Milton Friedman. Those individuals, more so than any others, expanded on Smith's discoveries and showed the practical implications of economic freedom for each individual worker.

Others who have carried on the battle to return power and influence from government to individuals are William Niskanen, Ed Crane, Peter Ferrara, Edwin Feulner, John Goodman, Jack Kemp, José Piñera, and J. Patrick Rooney. Their tireless efforts have helped to refine and publicize many of the ideas expressed in this book.

A special acknowledgment is necessary for Joe and Diane Bast of The Heartland Institute. In addition to their ongoing dedication to the principles of economic freedom, they were the driving force behind the publication of this book. Without their help and encouragement, the manuscript would not have seen the light of day.

Mentioning all these people in no way implies that they necessarily endorse or agree with the positions taken in this book. The specific content, as well as any shortcomings or errors in fact or in logic, are solely my responsibility.

Finally, I would like to acknowledge the contribution of my wife Maureen and my children Bob, Dennis, Alexis, and Tom. Their unfailing love and support mean more to me than they'll ever know.

PART ONE

Setting the Stage

INTRODUCTION

A popular way for an author to "get rich quick" is to write a book telling others how they can become millionaires. The objective of this book is different—it's far more ambitious. Its goal is to turn *every worker* in the country into a millionaire. And not just a millionaire in a world where a newspaper costs $10,000 and an economy car $2 million. In that world, being a millionaire wouldn't be worth much. This book spells out a plan that would turn every worker into a millionaire for *today's* world, in terms of today's money.

How quickly can this goal be accomplished? The answer will disappoint those in search of overnight millions. In this age of instant gratification, some readers will object to a plan that may take a lifetime to fulfill its objectives. Still, most people work their entire lives anyway. So why not consider a plan that promises financial security for all once the work is done? Some of the benefits of the plan outlined here will begin to show up immediately. Others will become more obvious as time goes on.

Also keep in mind that the book's objective is to turn *every* worker into a millionaire. This means that the *lowest*-paid worker retires with a million dollars in investable funds. Workers with average incomes become millionaires much sooner, and multi-millionaires by the time they retire.

Why aim at turning the United States into a nation of millionaires? After all, many of us are offended by blatant materialism, and wise enough to know that money isn't the most important thing in life. Some of us are concerned about the destruction of the environment or toxins in food and water. Others are troubled by poverty, hunger, and injustice. Still others worry about the breakdown of family values and the senseless violence and crime that pervade our cities.

These are all valid concerns, many of them worthy of books in their own right. It is important to recognize that each of these concerns would be more easily addressed, perhaps even eliminated, in a nation of millionaires.

Imagine an economy where everyone in the private, productive work force was building a small fortune just by doing whatever it is they are doing now. Imagine the effect this would have on those on welfare, or unemployed, or making their living from illegal activities. All would face strong incentives to be productive and obey the laws.

Instead of punishing welfare recipients or hunting down members of the underground economy, this book proposes to make the private, productive work force so attractive that no one can afford to be left out. The social and political implications of such a plan are mind-boggling.

Millionaires (or those on their way to becoming millionaires) are less likely to be found lurking in dark alleys waiting to victimize other citizens. They shouldn't have trouble paying for their health care. And they aren't likely to tolerate a dirty environment or toxins in their food.

So don't be fooled by the book's focus on income and wealth. In the end, it is about far more than creating millionaires. It is about restoring a society in which individuals are responsible for fulfilling their own needs and are financially able to do so. It is about a society in which individuals control their own destinies by taking responsibility for their futures. By doing so, they create far more than a nation of rich people. They enhance their dignity and self-esteem and, in the process, help to restore peace and harmony to a troubled society.

Proposals for major policy changes often create their own conflict and turmoil. Those who want to promote the agenda discussed in this book should do so with love for those who resist. Without love for one another, all the time and effort spent creating a nation of millionaires will be in vain.

Chapter 1

A SOCIETY IN DISTRESS

Crime, addiction, unwanted pregnancies, racial tension, child abuse, teen suicide—all have worsened in recent decades, affecting the lives of one family after another.

Empower America has collected information on the country's leading cultural indicators. What emerges is extremely unsettling:

- ✔ Since 1960, the rate at which crimes occur has increased by over 200 percent, and the rate for violent crimes is up almost 400 percent.
- ✔ Between 1972 and 1990, the rate of teen pregnancy increased over 100 percent.
- ✔ In 1960, 5 percent of all births were to unmarried women. In 1990, that figure had soared to 28 percent.
- ✔ In 1960, 23 percent of births to black women were to unmarried women. In 1990, that had risen to 65 percent.

✔ In 1960, 3.6 of every 100,000 teenagers committed suicide. In 1990, the number was 11.3.
✔ Single-parent families comprised 9 percent of the population in 1960, but 29 percent in 1991.
✔ The rate of child abuse rose from 101 cases per 10,000 children in 1976 to 420 cases in 1991.

Those readers old enough to remember what school was like in the 1940s and 1950s will recall such "serious" discipline problems as talking out of turn, chewing gum, running in the hallways, dress code infractions, and littering school grounds. Those problems, of course, pale in comparison to the drug and alcohol abuse, pregnancy, suicide, and violent crime that plague our elementary and secondary schools today.

These trends show a marked deterioration in the nation's social conditions. They demand that we take action. But what kind of action?

Too often, we respond only to the television special or newspaper exposé that calls immediate attention to some specific issue. Congress passes legislation to "solve" the problem, and then proceeds to the next challenge. One by one, each specific problem is dealt with, yet the number of problems grows. In the end, our real objective—that of a stable, peaceful, prosperous society—is further away than ever.

A general consensus favors reducing poverty and restoring traditional moral values. But there is no consensus—and a great deal of disagreement—about how to achieve those goals.

Poverty

On any given day, some observers of society's decline will identify our chief social problem as hunger, the elderly poor, homelessness, a lack of affordable health care, or some other specific deficiency. But the overriding problem is poverty. Focusing narrowly on one symptom of poverty diverts our attention from the core issue. It also ensures that any proposed solution will, at best, solve only a small part of the poverty problem. Developing a solution for only part of a problem can doom the solution to failure while often creating other problems.

In the late 1960s, the food stamp program was adopted to help feed the poor. Initially, the program appeared to be reasonably successful. Hungry people were fed. However, as the program continued, fraud and abuse began to overwhelm it. Today, it is not uncommon for food stamps to be exchanged for drugs or alcohol, or to buy premium foods that other shoppers cannot afford. Those observing such behavior quickly develop resentment and hostility toward those abusing the system, as well as toward the system itself for permitting such abuse.

In the 1970s, there was a great deal of concern over the elderly poor. To meet this concern, Congress legislated a substantial boost in Social Security benefits. The financial condition of the elderly poor improved, but the higher payroll taxes needed to pay for the improvement lowered the income of the middle class and the working poor. The "solution" to the problem of the elderly poor created serious economic problems for a whole generation of lower-income workers and their families.

And so it has gone. Efforts to relieve the various aspects of poverty have multiplied to the point where there are now eighty-four welfare programs at the federal level alone. The National Center for Policy Analysis (NCPA) estimates that total government welfare spending in 1994 was $350 billion (not including Social Security and Medicare). That is enough to pay each poor person $8,939 a year, or $35,756 for a family of four.

Simply dividing up government welfare expenses and giving the money to the poor is impractical for many reasons. No one believes the poor should be better off than the near-poor. Also, much of the money spent on welfare does not go to the poor. Detailed studies by the NCPA indicate that more than half of all families receiving at least one means-tested welfare benefit are in fact not poor. Even more disturbing, 41 percent of all families in poverty receive no means-tested benefit of any kind from the government.

At $350 billion, welfare expenditures in 1994 were greater than either Social Security retirement benefits or national defense spending. Those who propose spending even more to help the poor often are not aware of the magnitude of current spending. As government calls upon taxpayers to provide for the needs of others, the bill-payers often find themselves impoverished.

Government anti-poverty programs have failed miserably. Poverty today is worse than it was before the explosion in welfare programs. And the type of poverty that persists today is so disabling that we have coined a new phrase to describe its victims: the underclass.

Moral Values

Based strictly on income, many of today's poor would be considered wealthy by the standards of just two generations ago. Some of today's poor are students or interns, who sacrifice income today for more in the future. The lifestyle choices of others who are considered poor suggest that spending several times the current amount would not end their poverty. By contrast, many of those who earn an average wage today would be considered poor by the quality-of-life standards of the 1950s.

The condition of poverty involves more than income. It involves a way of living, a culture—a mind-set. Government programs to help the poor have spread the culture of poverty to a greater number of people than ever before. As a result, government welfare programs have merely replaced one aspect of poverty—the lack of material things—with others—a lack of character, ambition, and hope.

Poverty has existed at all times and in all places. According to the Bible, the poor will always be with us. But history shows that in some societies, rich and poor alike behaved with dignity and pride. They reared their children as responsible, hard-working citizens. As recently as the 1940s and '50s it was unnecessary to lock your doors in many neighborhoods. Those in need of a meal were often invited to share one with others. Today, both the rich and the poor are immersed in a breakdown of values and discipline that has led to broken families, chronic unemployment, crime, addiction, and needless suffering.

The deterioration began in the 1960s and has become worse in the years since. Not coincidentally, over the same period government has intensified its efforts to address each of the specific symptoms of poverty. In his book *Losing Ground*, sociologist Charles Murray highlights the relationship between the growth in government welfare programs and the development of a permanent underclass.

The roots of the problem go even deeper. In many instances a haphazard approach to solving problems has created new ones. Our narrowly targeted attempts to help the elderly poor, the hungry, the homeless, and other unfortunate members of society have lowered the incomes of the nation's workers and weakened the link between an individual's problems and the responsibility for solving them. Weakening that link has created a host of additional problems.

Only when individuals recognize their own responsibility for a problem and actively contribute to solving it, is a real solution possible. For government policies to play a constructive role in that process, they must help individuals to understand their responsibility for the problem at hand. Then, the policies must give each individual the incentive to solve his or her problem.

The First Step

Ironically, problems that may appear overwhelming when viewed in isolation—such as hunger, health care, education, and the environment— are actually more open to solution when they are understood to be symptoms of a single problem. Stepping back to view the forest, rather than focusing on the individual trees, gives us the necessary perspective to arrive at a meaningful solution.

Instead of taxing and vilifying those who succeed, a more promising approach is to allow *everyone* to succeed. As implausible as this might seem, a few relatively simple calculations show that the only obstacle standing between every American worker and incredible wealth is government. *The simple truth is that government institutions and policies are preventing most Americans from fully realizing their potential to become rich.* Changing those institutions and policies would enable even the lowest-paid workers to realize the type of wealth they now only dream about. The policy prescriptions outlined in this book make it possible for every worker in the country to become a millionaire.

The Numbers Game

The authors of the book *Living Hungry in America* spend a great deal of time debating how many people are hungry. But is that really the point? If there are 10 million people hungry, instead of 20 million, isn't 10 million still too many? Of course it is. But the authors' solution to the problem is to spend more "government" money addressing hunger, so naturally the number of hungry people is important to them. The more people affected by the problem, the more dollars they expected to funnel into their proposal. Arguing about numbers is really arguing over how many dollars should be transferred from one group to another to solve a problem.

When my estimates of the future value of workers' retirement accounts appeared in *The Wall Street Journal* on May 21, 1993, accountants and actuaries questioned the calculations. Some suggested that my numbers were too high, that the lowest-paid worker would have an income slightly lower than I projected. Others said my numbers were too low. They were all right—because there are hundreds of ways to calculate the impact of any particular policy change. (For those who like to play with numbers, I've included an appendix filled with various calculations.)

The debate about the number of hungry people exhausted the energy of both advocates and critics of government hunger relief programs. Similarly, the debate over how rich is rich and precisely how much each retiree receives in benefits only distracts us from our ultimate goal. Such a debate is diversionary and should be recognized as such. Whether the lowest-paid worker ends up with a few hundred thousand dollars or a few million dollars is not nearly as important as the fact that substantial gains can be realized by all workers.

The reforms discussed in this book will go a long way toward making the next generation financially independent. More importantly, they will determine the essence of the type of nation America will become. They will mean the difference between a nation of individuals who are proud, independent, and financially secure, and a nation of people dependent on the largess or private agendas of others. A nation of dependents includes individuals who are forever pleading with their politicians to give back a small portion of what they themselves produced. A nation of independent individuals is vastly different. Its members realize that they, and not their government, are fully responsible for their own well-being.

The real debate is over nothing less than responsibility versus dependency.

Chapter 2

RESPONSIBILITY,
NOT DEPENDENCY

For two centuries, the United States has been a beacon of hope for the rest of the world. That hope is based on what was once a novel and untested idea: that citizens could successfully govern themselves. The United States has proven democracy so successful that it has become the only legitimate model of political organization. But democracy was only one part of the Founding Fathers' unique experiment. They believed not only that individuals can be responsible for governing themselves . . . but also that individuals *have a responsibility* to provide for their own needs. This second idea was every bit as important to them as the first. True freedom involves not only people electing their political leaders, but also people accepting responsibility for their own needs. Only when individuals provide for their own needs are they able to develop into mature, responsible members of society. Only then are they truly free and independent.

Government's Duty

As viewed by the Founding Fathers, government has certain responsibilities. First and foremost is the obligation to provide an environment that enables individuals to achieve their highest potential, in terms of their contributions to society and in terms of the rewards they receive for those contributions. Creating this environment involves four things: low tax burdens, free markets, protection of property rights, and a stable currency with which to conduct business.

Low taxes make it easier for people to provide for their own needs by letting them keep their hard-earned income. Free markets help maximize output, and thus earnings, by providing vital information about the value of goods and services. Markets are free when government is limited and individuals are primarily responsible for their own needs. Property rights protect the accumulation of assets from confiscation. Without such rights, individuals would have little incentive to create wealth. A stable currency is needed to provide reliable information about transactions and to prevent government from usurping resources by devaluing the currency.

In recent decades, government has obviously failed in its obligation to provide an economic environment in which individuals can achieve independence and assume responsibility. High tax rates, the seemingly unconstrained growth in government, interference with markets, a withering away of property rights, and persistent inflation have placed substantial barriers in the way of achieving independence. As the ability of individuals to provide for their own needs is eroded, economic, moral, and cultural deterioration accelerate. If recent trends persist, insecurity, injustice, and crime will become even more pervasive.

Recent attempts to document the deterioration in social and cultural values highlight what many people already recognize. A growing number of the nation's individuals are adopting values totally at odds with what is acceptable in an advanced civilized society.

Why People Behave As They Do

This leads to an important question: Why do individuals behave as they do?

Behavior is shaped by three things: values, incentives, and information. An individual's values are formed from the lessons provided by parents, teachers, friends, relatives, religious leaders, and even government. A government that is corrupt and immoral is certain to be a negative influence on its people. A judicial system that renders the concept of law meaningless by interpreting it to conform to the latest social theory hastens the erosion of moral values. When those charged with interpreting the law mold it to reflect their own preferences, they undermine respect for the law and promote lawlessness.

The inclination toward criminal activity can be overcome by a strong system of social and moral values. Still, the more society's institutions reflect a lack of values, the greater the erosion is likely to be among its people. When a society adopts policies making it more difficult to respect moral values, it dilutes those values.

Behavior is also influenced by incentives. While individuals don't always realize it, they often make decisions in response to economic pressures. For example, when an individual has little to lose, the potential gains from criminal activity seem relatively high and the penalties for getting caught appear relatively low. Applying such cost-benefit analysis to crime may seem crude, but it is both appropriate and accurate. The greater the rewards from an activity, and the lower its costs, the more people will tend to engage in it.

Once a nation in which crime did not pay, the United States has become one in which crime often pays handsomely. According to the National Center for Policy Analysis, for example, in the mid-1950s the typical criminal served 22.5 days for a serious crime. That fell to 12 days by 1964, and to just 8 days by 1990. In 1990, a murderer could expect to serve just 1.8 years in prison; a rapist, 60 days; a robber, 23 days; and

17

someone who committed an aggravated assault, 6.4 days.

The commission of a crime can be a rational economic choice if the expected loss is minimal. If individuals have little income and assets to lose, and if their expected punishment is fairly mild, more of them can be expected to commit crimes. As taxes take a larger and larger bite out of people's paychecks, the ability of lower-income workers to support themselves—not to mention their families—is undermined. As the rewards for legitimate work decline, the pressures for criminal activity become even greater.

On the opposite end of the income spectrum, it doesn't make much sense for a millionaire to engage in criminal activity. Relative to his or her prospects in the legitimate economy, the potential benefits of crime are small. Moreover, the cost of getting caught is enormous: considerable lost income for time spent in court or in jail, lost assets for compensating the victims of the crime and paying court costs, and social rejection by family, friends, and the community at large.

This doesn't mean that the rich are more virtuous than the poor. Many who are poor have the social and moral upbringing to avoid the temptations of criminal activity. By contrast, those who are rich and without principles do commit crimes, but they are seldom the random, violent crimes that have become commonplace in recent years. When individuals see themselves as being or becoming rich, they have strong incentives to avoid crime, particularly violent crime.

Policies That Promote Dependency

Government policies that promote dependency seriously undermine values and incentives. These policies encourage irresponsible behavior by providing misleading information about its consequences. The influence of such policies extends well beyond the welfare population. Collectively, they have produced a nation of individuals dependent on government.

Policies that foster dependency permeate almost every aspect of our lives: retirement, health care, the legal system, welfare, and, perhaps most importantly, education. Instead of encouraging individuals to accept responsibility for their lives and their decisions, government policies discourage such behavior.

As government takes on more responsibility for the problems of its citizens, individuals feel less responsibility to provide for themselves. Moreover, their ability to do so is significantly reduced. Each time government is called on to fulfill a need, there is a cost. The more needs government attempts to fulfill, the higher the costs. Since individuals are the ones who pay for government programs, they are inevitably left with fewer resources to fulfill their own needs.

It is instructive to realize what has happened to the typical family's income over time. The most meaningful way to measure income is after taxes and after inflation. This measure is called *real spendable earnings*. It measures the amount of money a family has available to live on. The federal government used to calculate a similar figure, but it stopped doing so sometime around 1980 because the trend was so depressing.

Despite the lack of official figures, it is possible to estimate the trend in after-tax family income. Consider the "typical family," one whose yearly income is right in the middle of all families (that is, there are as many families earning more as earning less). After-tax income trends can be plotted for several types of families: two-income families, single-parent families, etc. Since cultural changes and financial hardships led many families to shift to two wage earners in recent decades (thus making it difficult to plot income trends over a long period of time), it is most useful to focus on the typical family where only the husband works.

In today's dollars, that family earned after-tax income of $31,000 in 1972, but just $26,000 in 1993. (See the graph on page 20.) In that twenty-one-year period, the family's after-tax take-home pay fell by 16 percent. As government has taken a progressively greater share of family income, families are left with less money for their basic needs, and they are made more dependent on government.

Dependency may be appropriate for young children. But as they grow and mature, even children must be given more responsibility. If they are not, they remain dependent upon their parents and never become responsible adults.

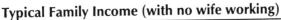

Typical Family Income (with no wife working)

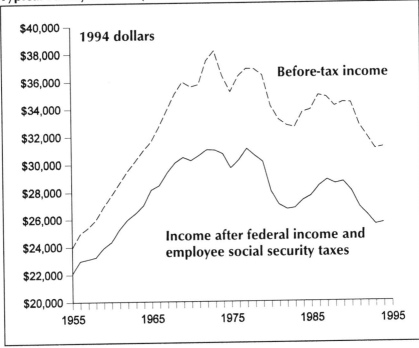

Similarly, a nation where a significant portion of the population behaves as dependents can never be a great nation. It can be only a nation of individuals who have failed to attain maturity and independence; a nation of individuals who will insist on blaming others for their problems; a nation of individuals who constantly look to government, as a child looks to a parent, to solve its problems.

When a parent solves a problem for a child, the child isn't always better off. While the immediate problem may be addressed, too often another problem is created. The child has been made more dependent than ever on the actions of the parent. Far wiser is the parent who sympathizes with the child's problem, talks it over, and tries to explain how the child might solve the problem. The child begins to learn problem-solving techniques and takes the first steps toward true independence and maturity.

In the United States, government increasingly has taken on the role of parent. Unfortunately, it has done a miserable job with its "children." Almost without fail, government has hindered the development of independence and maturity. Politicians have developed programs to "solve" the problems of their needy constituents, instead of providing the tools and assistance to enable individuals to solve their own problems.

Social Security

Our current system of Social Security gives government the power to decide how much of an "allowance" retirees should receive and how they must behave to receive it. Those who choose to work past the normal retirement age can be punished with lower allowances. Spouses who never worked may be rewarded with greater benefits than those who worked full-time. Single persons who die upon reaching retirement age have all of their allowance taken away.

By creating a class of dependent retirees, Social Security has led to resentment, indignity, and a sense of frustration and betrayal. It has caused retirees to form political pressure groups to defend what they have earned and what they thought they had been promised. Born of a program based on dependency, these political groups tend to act like children. They insist that their immediate demands be met and ignore the longer-term implications of maintaining the present system. Like children, these groups often refuse even to listen to any suggestions for altering the system.

Welfare

The tendency of government programs to create dependents extends most destructively to the current system of welfare. Unlike retirees, who have already lived productive, independent lives, welfare recipients have their lives and the lives of their children influenced by the policies of dependency. At virtually every turn, the present welfare system works to keep those who are poor from overcoming their condition. Any of the poor who decide to work and accumulate assets face the prospect of losing food stamps, housing allowances, educational grants, and a host of other potential benefits.

Instead of providing the poor with the means to solve their problems, government welfare programs aim at solving their problems for them. By penalizing constructive behavior such as thrift, deferred gratification, or the exercising of foresight regarding the future, the present system makes it extremely difficult for the poor to gain true independence.

Health Care

For many at the lower end of the income scale, the health care system creates a major incentive against legitimate work and accumulating assets. Those individuals who have few assets and little income, or those who are in prison, can receive unlimited free or nearly free treatment for serious illnesses under various government programs. Those who work hard for a living must pay heavily for the same services.

The public education system, legal system, and regulatory system also create dependency. Through them, government is called upon to educate children, ensure that the injured receive compensation, and restore or maintain the environment. All are important objectives. But a healthy society is one that provides the institutional arrangements necessary to help people solve their own problems.

A Nation of Dependents

Over the past several decades, a cycle of dependency has been created. Government policies have eroded the responsibility of individuals to provide for their own well-being, and taxation has severely limited their financial ability to do so. Government policies have replaced a nation of free, independent individuals with a nation of individuals dependent on government.

A nation of dependents can be neither great nor prosperous. To reverse the deterioration in today's society, we must fundamentally change government policies. Our efforts must be aimed at the heart of the problem, changing incentives and information to reinforce each individual's responsibility for shaping his or her own life.

Such changes in government policy will strengthen traditional values and promote true freedom and responsibility among the greatest number of people. And, as the following chapters will show, they also will have an important side effect: they will create a nation of millionaires.

PART TWO

Long-Term Planning

Chapter 3

SOCIAL SECURITY: REVERSING BANKRUPTCY

Of all the government policies that foster dependency while undermining prosperity, none is more insidious than Social Security. The Social Security system is already bankrupt. Its coming collapse will carry with it the retirement dreams of several generations. Unless we address the fundamental problems of Social Security soon, working Americans will have to pay ever-higher taxes to support those who have retired, and retirees will have to accept benefits far lower than they have been promised.

During one of the darkest periods in American history—the Civil War—fathers fought sons in a war that turned family against family. In a similar way, Social Security threatens to turn children against their parents in an ongoing dispute over control of retirement income.

Most older Americans have genuinely positive feelings toward the present Social Security system. Many have parents or grandparents whose retirements were made more financially secure as a result of the present system. They are understandably reluctant to change anything that seems to be working. Unfortunately, their fond memories soon will be gone.

The public supports Social Security today because few understand how the system really works. The greater their understanding, the more apparent it becomes that a government that epitomizes fiscal irresponsibility should never be allowed to control something as important as people's retirement funds.

Social Security Is a Ponzi Scheme

The fundamental problem with Social Security is that it is based on the principles of a Ponzi or pyramid scheme. In such schemes, the original investors get paid off with funds from a second group of investors. The returns decrease for each successive group of investors until finally, the later ones realize what a bad deal it is and the system goes broke. Ponzi schemes are generally illegal, unless they are run by government.

When Social Security was established in 1935, it operated as a fully funded system. All the taxes collected for the program were used to pay future benefits. That reasonable requirement was necessary for Congressional approval.

In a fully funded retirement system, contributions are not spent on current enjoyment, but are saved for the future. True *investment* takes place, and the economy grows faster than it would without the investment. In a fully funded system, the benefits that people eventually receive are the result of extra growth stimulated by extra savings. In the truest sense, people *earn* their retirement benefits, because without the additional investment, those benefits would not have been available.

Most Americans believe that Social Security continues to operate as a fully funded system. They believe that their "contributions" to the system are invested for their retirement, or that at least some portion of the funds is saved for their future use. Nothing could be further from the truth.

In 1939, the Social Security system was changed to allow benefits to be paid from current contributions. Gradually, Social Security became a pay-as-you-go system. Before long, every dollar paid into the system was immediately spent, either to pay benefits for current retirees or to pay for some other government program.

Like the workers under a fully funded system, today's workers must sacrifice to pay Social Security taxes. However, the taxes paid by today's workers are not invested for their future use, but are spent immediately on benefits for those who are already retired. For today's workers, Social Security is worse than no retirement program at all: It demands that workers make payments into the system, thereby reducing their ability to save for their own retirements. Worse still, it does not invest the payments they make, yet promises them future benefits, thereby reducing their incentive to save for their own retirements.

Many Social Security recipients believe that their benefits are the direct result of their years of labor and sacrifice. That would be true if Social Security operated as a fully funded retirement system. But with pay-as-you-go, there is no direct relationship between contributions and benefits. Two people working and contributing the same amount all their lives can end up with very different benefits, depending on their marital status, earnings in retirement, and other factors. Under certain conditions, a person who marries several times can have his or her current spouse, as well as all previous spouses, receive spousal benefits. The system is so complex that no one can know in advance how much in Social Security benefits an individual will receive.

Many Social Security recipients also believe that their contributions to the system guarantee them a retirement income. In fact, however, they have no legal claim to their Social Security benefits. In 1960, the Supreme Court ruled in *Flemming v. Nestor* that workers do not have any accrued property rights associated with Social Security. Social Security benefits are governed entirely by the whim of Congress, which was clever enough to make sure its members had a generous pension system in addition to Social Security. When most workers and retirees learn that the government has not invested one penny of their money for retirement, and that they have absolutely no legal claim to their previous contributions, they react with shock and disbelief.

Social Security is a system created by politicians with little regard for either its economic impact or equity. It is a system designed to reward retirees at the expense of workers. In one of the debates marking an earlier stop-gap plan to save Social Security, one Congressman said to his staff, "I don't care what has to be done, just make certain it lasts until I retire."

A Bankrupt System

Those who defend Social Security insist that it remains solvent. They fail to understand the meaning of bankruptcy. Social Security is solvent only under the assumption of some combination of significant tax increases and benefit reductions. No one can deny that doubling Social Security taxes and raising the retirement age to 90 would make Social Security solvent. This is not unlike saying that a bankrupt firm would be solvent if only its revenues were higher and its costs lower!

Since the government forces new workers to pay for the benefits of retirees, the Social Security system won't declare bankruptcy in the traditional sense. Rather, tax burdens on workers will continue to rise while retirement benefits will be reduced. That process has already begun.

The typical family today pays more in Social Security taxes than in income taxes. Yet benefits have been falling. Taxes on Social Security income have been increased twice, while the retirement age has been raised from 65 to 67. Changes of this type will become even more common as taxes are further increased and benefits further reduced to ensure the system's "solvency."

The pay-as-you-go nature of the present system made it possible to give the first generation of retirees a tremendous return on their payments. After all, there were relatively few retirees and a large labor force to support them. With each generation, however, the returns have declined. Those retiring now are being promised roughly a zero percent return on the money they paid in. And they will achieve this only if there are no further cuts in benefits. Most workers who retire twenty years from now will receive less than they paid in, even if all promised benefits are paid. And, since the currently promised benefits are far too generous for the economy to support, they will not be paid. If the Social Security system is not changed, we can expect to see an ugly battle between workers and retirees over how much more workers will have to pay and how much less retirees will receive.

The Coming Collapse

Today, there are 3.2 workers contributing to Social Security for each retiree. As the baby boomers retire, that ratio will fall. By the year 2030, the system's trustees assume that there will be 2.0 workers for each retiree. Some analysts have calculated that Social Security taxes alone would have to be 30 to 40 percent just to pay for the next generation's benefits. In Europe, where the demise of the pay-as-you-go system is further along, rates are already at these levels. In Belgium, the combined employer-employee social security tax is 47 percent. (By contrast, in the U.S. today the combined rate is 15.3 percent.) Once these taxes are added to the others, it will be a wonder if anyone shows up for work! Moreover, as medical breakthroughs extend life expectancy, the system collapses more quickly. It doesn't take much imagination to see why a recent opinion poll found that more young people believe they'll see a UFO than a Social Security check.

31

Each year the trustees of the Social Security system issue a status report. Those reports have been consistently irresponsible. In their 1996 report, the trustees estimate that the retirement and disability trust funds will be sufficient to enable the timely payment of benefits for the next thirty years. The trustees have always been confident about the financial health of Social Security because they view it as independent of both the government and the economy. From their perspective, the system had $500 billion in assets at the end of 1995 and is expected to generate surpluses of close to $30 billion for the next ten years, thereby ensuring its viability.

However, Social Security is inextricably tied to the rest of the government. The current surpluses are being spent on other government programs. In return, the Treasury sends the trust fund IOUs, which the trustees view as the system's assets. At the end of 1995, the Social Security retirement and disability funds listed "assets" of about $500 billion—just over one year's obligations. However, for the system to use those assets, the Treasury would have to repay its IOUs. The only way it could do this would be to sell more debt, cut other government programs, or raise taxes.

The trustees acknowledge that problems will be accentuated as the baby boomers reach retirement age. Under their most likely scenario, benefits are expected to exceed contributions within fifteen years. But under their pessimistic scenario, this occurs in just four years.

The trustees' solution for covering any shortfall is a tax increase. When the trustees are told that higher taxes would mean less economic activity, and therefore an even greater shortfall, they respond by saying that such problems exceed their responsibility.

If the present system is not altered in some fundamental way, government will have to raise taxes dramatically while cutting Social Security benefits and postponing the retirement age. Each of these moves represents an explicit recognition of the system's bankruptcy.

A Bad Deal

There can be no doubt that the present Social Security system does a gross injustice to future generations. While there has been much wailing over the effect of budget deficits on future generations, little has been said about how the Social Security system robs them of their future financial security. There can be no justification other than ignorance for treating our children this way.

Even if Social Security could deliver the benefits it promises, it would be a bad deal. A study by the Cato Institute indicates that a worker born in 1950 who invested his payroll taxes in either bonds or stocks would be far better off than he is with Social Security. An investment in bonds yielded two to three times the monthly benefits of Social Security. An investment in stocks did four to six times better. For a low-wage worker, investing payroll taxes in stocks would have meant a monthly retirement benefit of $2,490, compared to a $631 Social Security payment. For a high-wage worker, monthly benefits could have been $9,972 instead of $1,562.

The present generation is paying dearly for the mistakes made by those who established the Social Security system. If those mistakes are not corrected, future generations will suffer even greater losses.

The Solution: Privatize

Fortunately, there is a solution to the present Social Security mess. Instead of pitting one generation against another, impoverishing both in the process, privatizing Social Security would enable the lowest-paid worker in the United States to retire with over $380,000 in investable assets. Social Security privatization is a plan that has proven itself in other countries. And it is the only plan that can ensure that future retirees will receive the benefits they have been promised.

Chile provides a model for privatizing Social Security. In 1981, Chilean employees were given the choice of continuing their participation in the government-sponsored, U.S.-style social security system or opting for a private alternative. Those who chose the latter received a government "recognition" bond reflecting their prior contributions to social security. The bond earns a real interest rate of 4 percent.

In addition, employees who opted for the private pension system received an immediate increase in their wages (from their employers) equal to the amount those employers were paying in social security taxes. That helps to expose the myth that payroll taxes are somehow paid by the company. Economic research confirms that employers simply reduce wages to offset the impact of payroll taxes.

To implement the private social security plan, each Chilean worker selected a pension fund manager from a group approved by the government. Employers send 13 percent of each employee's salary to that manager: ten percent for the worker's retirement fund, and the rest for purchasing a death and disability insurance policy and paying the fund manager.

Between 1981 and 1993, the average annual real return to the private pension funds was 13.7 percent. The typical Chilean employee (who earns the equivalent of $5,400 a year) now holds a pension fund valued at approximately $7,000. In addition, the typical employee has roughly $14,000 worth of recognition bonds from contributions to the prior system. All told, the typical Chilean worker has roughly $21,000—almost four times average yearly income—in his or her retirement account.

Consider by contrast the typical U.S. family. In 1993, its annual income was roughly $38,000. Its total wealth, including the net value of its retirement accounts, homes, insurance policies, and stocks, amounted to roughly $50,000. While the typical Chilean worker has a retirement account alone that is roughly equal to four years of income, the typical U.S. family's *total* wealth is roughly equal to only *sixteen months* of income.

34

The comparison between the assets of U.S. workers and their Chilean counterparts will soon be even more dramatic. In Chile, the effect of compounding is just starting to take hold. In less than ten years, given extremely conservative assumptions, the typical Chilean worker's pension account will be worth $60,000 in today's dollars. At some point in the next decade, the typical Chilean worker will have more wealth in a retirement account than the entire net worth of his or her American counterpart.

The success of Chile's privatized social security system has become so obvious that all of its neighbors have moved to privatize their own systems. Argentina, Colombia, and Peru already have made the transition to private retirement systems. Five other Latin American countries are planning to privatize their systems in the next year or two. Those nations closest to Chile can see the benefits first-hand. They don't want to be left out.

What Privatization Would Mean for Us

Chile's experience merely hints at what could be accomplished in a relatively high-income country. In the United States, the potential for creating both wealth and financial security is incredible.

Assume, for example, that a 17-year-old worker, earning a wage of $4.25 an hour ($8,840 a year), were to put 10 percent of that income into a retirement account each year. If those funds earned 6 percent per year (1 percent less than historical returns to stocks after inflation), *and the worker never got a raise,* he or she would retire at age 67 with over a quarter of a million dollars.

That, however, is only the beginning of the story. Since a private pension system would actually *invest* workers' retirement funds, economic growth, real incomes, and returns to investment would increase dramatically. Just as no one in the United States today would think of working for $1.50 an hour (the minimum-wage equivalent in 1946), no one fifty years from now should think of working for $4.25 an hour. If, as a result of increased economic growth, the lowest-paid worker were to receive wage increases of just 2 percent a year, he or she would retire with over $380,000 in investable assets.

Under the same assumptions—10 percent contributions into a retirement account earning 6 percent per year, and economic growth sufficient to guarantee 2 percent annual wage increases—a worker currently earning $500 a week ($12.50 an hour for a forty-hour week) would retire with a million dollars in investable assets. Since well over half of all American families today earn over $500 a week, this single change in public policy would leave them with over a million dollars in investable funds by the time they retire.

Is it possible to move from the current, destructive Social Security system to a fully funded private system at this point in the pyramid? It is. Before its transformation, the Chilean system was worse than ours.

The United States could begin the transition by giving all workers the opportunity to opt out of Social Security. Most of those now retired or nearing retirement would probably choose to remain in the current system. Those who remain, including all current retirees, should be given property rights to their retirement benefits—rights that cannot be rescinded whenever a new group of politicians decides to change tax rates or retirement ages. If government policies are to reflect traditional values, then promises must be kept.

Workers who opt out of the current system would receive government bonds. The value of those bonds would be set to ensure that no one opting out of the system is worse off financially than they would have been had they remained. The youngest workers, who have contributed little to the current Social Security system, would receive little or no payment from the government system. But they are the ones who would benefit most from a lifetime of private savings.

Obstacles to Privatization

The principal obstacle to privatizing Social Security is the problem of financing benefits for current retirees while enabling the next generation to opt out of the system. Reversing a pyramid scheme is never easy. Just as there was a gain to the first generation in the system, there will be a cost to the generation that corrects the problem. However, the cost becomes even greater the longer the present system continues.

Fortunately, since the economy is dynamic, the costs are not nearly as burdensome as they appear. Social Security payments for retirement and disability were $340 billion in 1995; they are expected to be roughly $577 billion in 2005. It is that first ten-year period that presents the greatest difficulty in the transition back to a fully funded system. Beyond the first two decades, government expenditures for benefits would drop as individuals begin to retire with their own funds and today's retirees pass on.

In the initial years of the transition, the federal government would have to continue spending $350 to $400 billion each year for retirement benefits. At the same time, the government could lose virtually all of the retirement "contributions" from its present Social Security system, depending on the number of workers who choose to opt out. Hence, in the first year of the transition, government spending would remain the same, while its revenues could drop by as much as $400 billion.

It is this drop in revenues that presents the greatest hurdle to privatizing Social Security. The prospect of adding $400 billion or more to the deficit is enough for many to dismiss the proposal out of hand.

Those concerned about traditional federal deficits often fail to recognize the importance of future debt. In the case of Social Security, the present value of all future unfunded benefits is estimated to be $11 trillion. Even if the traditional budget deficit were eliminated by the year 2002 (as many politicians have promised), Social Security liabilities will increase the national debt by about $300 billion in that single year.

In a recent lecture, titled "The Missing Piece in Policy Analysis: Social Security Reform," economist Martin Feldstein estimates that the present value of the gains from privatizing Social Security would be almost twice the value of Social Security liabilities. In other words, the improvement in economic performance from privatizing Social Security would wipe out the existing unfunded liabilities with billions of dollars to spare.

Where Are Our Priorities?

As we evaluate proposed changes to Social Security, as well as other economic policy decisions, it is important to focus on what the policy is supposed to accomplish. If our objective is to create a system that enables the greatest number of people to attain the greatest amount of income and wealth, then privatizing Social Security accomplishes this objective.

Unfortunately, many policy analysts suggest that other objectives are more important than creating wealth and prosperity. To some, balancing the traditional federal budget is the ultimate objective of economic policy. They believe that balancing this budget is such an important accomplishment that it will somehow assure that prosperity will follow.

But reducing the federal deficit or even balancing the budget will not ensure prosperity. President Jimmy Carter reduced the federal budget deficit more successfully than many other presidents, yet almost every measure of economic performance deteriorated during his tenure.

Balancing the budget simply means fully funding all government programs. But fully funding a bad program is no way to achieve prosperity. It is far more important to evaluate the *usefulness* of federal programs than to be preoccupied with *funding* them. The current Social Security program impoverishes current retirees and future generations. It does this by taking income that should be saved and invested for the future and spending it today. A constructive solution to the Social Security problem would correct this flaw—not find a way to fund it.

All of the arguments used today to avoid privatizing Social Security in the U.S. were also used by those who opposed the new Chilean system. Critics argued that the increased government debt would reduce private savings. They argued that an increase in debt associated with the transition would mean higher interest rates. And they claimed that workers wouldn't tolerate paying for two retirements—their own as well as that of existing retirees.

It is important to recognize that the transition to a private social security system will not lead to miraculous changes—for good or for evil—overnight. In fact, during the first year of the new system, there would be little meaningful change. The deficit in the Social Security account would be as much as $400 billion, and the federal deficit might increase by an additional $30 billion (this represents the annual Social Security surplus currently spent on other government programs). Without Social Security contributions to income, there would be great pressure to cut spending. Just as families must adjust to a loss in income, government would have to do the same.

Clearly, it would be in the public's best interest to cut wasteful government spending as much as possible, or to sell federal assets to offset much, if not all, of the lost revenue during the transition. However, even in the worst case—where all the temporary increase in debt was financed by borrowing—the added debt would be *entirely* offset by almost $400 billion a year that the nation's workers would put into their own retirement accounts.

The dynamic impact of a private social security system builds as each year goes by. Chile's experience shows that private savings would tend to grow relative to public liabilities. In addition, the increased returns from private retirement accounts will offer workers far more funds for retirement than they ever could have attained under the public program. As workers see their retirement accounts grow, a sense of pride and accomplishment develops. Individuals recognize that they alone are responsible for their retirement. The relationship between a lifetime of work and economic security in retirement becomes more apparent than ever before. Just as owning one's home instills a special sense of pride, owning a retirement fund instills a sense of security and financial insight that cannot be obtained under the government-run system that now exists.

The political establishment will insist that the transitional debt makes a private system unthinkable. But it is important to remember that this is the same group that gave the public a pyramid scheme for retirement while assuring themselves of an incredibly generous retirement package.

The real implication of shifting funds out of the hands of politicians and into the hands of workers is that doing so shifts the levers of power. Those who own or control assets have power. That power now resides with politicians. Privatizing Social Security would shift that power into the hands of ordinary workers.

Imagining Privatization

Imagine the social and economic implications of allowing low-income workers to accumulate hundreds of thousands of dollars. With enormous visible rewards for legitimate work, the nation's moral and social structure would change dramatically. By increasing the rewards for legitimate work, reliance on government programs and illegal activities would be far more costly. Every day spent on welfare or unemployment insurance, every day spent earning illegal or unreported income, becomes a day when funds are not added to the worker's retirement account. Illegitimate work and idleness would become far more costly and far less attractive than they now appear.

When the lowest-paid workers see their fortunes grow, the economic system itself would provide enormous pressure for reducing crime and developing more independent and responsible workers. It is interesting to speculate about how many senseless crimes reported on the nightly news and the front pages of newspapers could be prevented by this one relatively simple change in public policy.

Our generation could leave no more important legacy than a system that allows future generations to fund their own retirement. And, since the lowest-paid workers in the country would be able to retire with over $380,000 in investable assets, the new system would go a long way toward creating a nation of millionaires.

Charting Our Progress

The tables and graphs at the end of each chapter, beginning with this one, show the impact of each proposed policy change on the financial assets of the lowest-paid worker. Each reform affects not only the worker's annual income, but also the funds that accumulate in his or her retirement account. I calculate the benefits that each person is likely to receive from reforms simply by dividing estimates of annual national savings by the number of people in the working population. This "average benefit" is then added to the income and/or savings of the lowest-paid worker.

It may be objected that some of the reforms outlined in the following chapters won't benefit people earning low incomes as much as they would benefit people who earn more. That may be true in some cases. But in other cases, the poor will benefit *more* than the wealthy.

For example, while the wealthy may benefit more from the reform of our legal system (chapter 8), the poor are more likely to benefit from reforms to education (chapter 5). Overall, there is no reason to believe that low-income people would receive less than the *average* per-person benefit from all six of the recommended reforms. Nevertheless, the reader should be aware that each estimate of benefits is only an approximation, and that benefits will vary from person to person.

The table below shows, in the left column, the annual income of a 17-year-old worker making $4.25 an hour, and the amount of money in the worker's private retirement account at the end of the first year of his or her working life. The right column shows the worker's annual income and retirement account funds at the end of his or her working life.

On the following page, the first graph shows how the worker's income would rise over his or her lifetime. The second shows the amount of money that lowest-paid worker would accumulate in a retirement account if 10 percent of his or her salary were invested each year and earned a real return of 6 percent.

Economic Impact on Lowest-Paid Worker: Social Security Privatization			
Annual Income at Age 17	$8,840	Annual Income at Age 67	$23,800
Retirement Account at Age 17	$908	Retirement Account at Age 67	$380,000

Annual Income of Lowest-Paid Worker
(assuming wage increases of 2 percent a year)

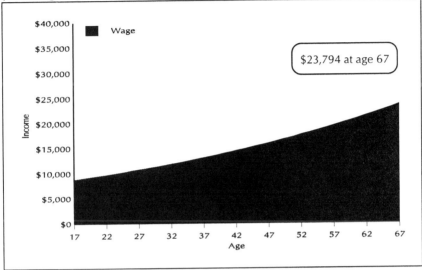

$23,794 at age 67

Retirement Assets of Lowest-Paid Worker:
Privatization of Social Security

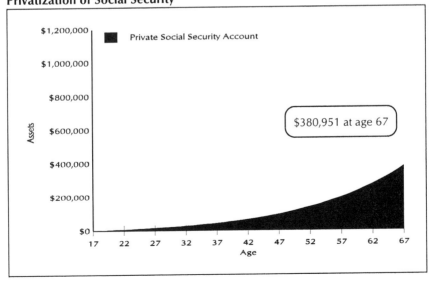

$380,951 at age 67

Chapter 4

EMPOWERING PATIENTS

Just as Social Security erodes individual responsibility for retirement, the nation's health care system erodes individual responsibility for health care. Today, 80 percent of the money individuals spend for health care is somebody else's money. And, since somebody else controls the dollars, decisions regarding doctors, treatment methods, and place of treatment are increasingly being taken out of the hands of individual patients.

Serious consequences result from taking health care responsibility away from individuals and placing it in the hands of a regulated bureaucracy. Increasingly, decisions regarding medical treatment are being made not by doctors in consultation with their patients, but by a government agent or some insurance firm. These decisions affect not only the quality of medical care, but also the cost. Recent experiments show patients to be much more cost-conscious health care shoppers when they are given primary responsibility for their health care decisions.

Because patients today have little reason to be cost-conscious, much of the money being spent on health care is wasted: not only on tests or treatments that are unnecessary, but even more on services that are unnecessarily expensive. Since expenditures for health care are close to $1 trillion a year, it is likely that anywhere from $300 to $500 billion a year represents pure waste. While politicians moan and groan over the impact of a $200 billion federal deficit, an equal or greater amount is being wasted away in health care expenditures alone.

Patient Power

The main problem with the current health care system is the lack of individual responsibility for health care spending. The present health care system isn't the result of some conscious plan or the free play of market forces. Rather, it evolved gradually from a series of government mistakes.

The evolution of our health care system, and what should be done to address its failures, is the subject of the book *Patient Power*, by John Goodman and Gerald Musgrave. *Patient Power* is "must" reading for anyone wishing to understand the health care system's complexities. It is also a source for many of the ideas in this chapter.

Traditionally, decisions regarding health care in the United States were made by individuals. That began to change, however, after the imposition of wage and price controls during World War II. Those controls prevented employers from offering higher wages to attract workers, so they began offering health insurance instead. Because it was exempt from taxes, this new benefit became more attractive as tax rates increased over the years.

When Is Insurance Not Insurance?

The health insurance that employers offer isn't insurance in the traditional sense. Traditional insurance pays a predetermined sum for unforeseen, risky events. Medical insurance, by contrast, is best described as prepayment for spending on medical services. When health insurance kicks in, it does not pay a predetermined amount, as is the case with life or homeowner's insurance. Rather, the payment depends on the type and number of medical services chosen by the insured.

Goodman and Musgrave show how this system is inherently unstable and goes through several stages. The first stage encourages people to overspend on medical services, because they are spending "the insurance company's" money. That overspending leads to the second stage, where the cost of providing health care services increases rapidly. This, in turn, evolves into the third stage, where efforts to contain costs lead to government control and a deterioration in the quality of medical services. President Clinton's 1993 attempt at sweeping health care reform, and what some observers refer to as the "managed care crisis" in health care today, offer strong evidence that our country's health care system has reached this third stage.

Government Moves In

As if the development of third-party health care financing through insurance companies were not bad enough, in the mid-1960s government became more involved in the whole process. Early in that decade, government accounted for less than 5 percent of all spending on health care. By 1992, however, government controlled 41 percent of every dollar spent on health care. Medicare accounted for 17 percent, Medicaid 14 percent, and other public costs 10 percent.

The heavy involvement of government in any activity inevitably means more bureaucracy, paperwork, and regulation. A study of the operating budgets of seventy hospitals found that their administrative costs increased by an average of 90 percent between 1983 and 1990. The study attributed the increase primarily to increased regulatory obligations.

The two main avenues of government involvement in health care are the Medicare and Medicaid programs. Medicare is designed to assist the elderly and the disabled, while Medicaid is designed to assist the poor. Both programs are growing rapidly. In 1993, 35 million people were covered by Medicare, and an additional 31 million were covered by Medicaid. Through these two programs alone, roughly 26 percent of the U.S. population receives government-paid health care.

Perhaps the most startling thing about government health care programs is that they have failed in their main objective: to make health care less expensive for the people they serve. Elderly Americans are now spending more than twice as much (after inflation) of their out-of-pocket money on health care as they did before Medicare was introduced. Medicare causes the elderly to demand more health care; the extra demand raises health care prices; and the higher prices cause Medicare spending to increase even more. Health care price increases have become so great that 60 cents out of every dollar spent on health care is eaten away by higher prices.

Medicaid figures show that nearly two out of every ten Americans are considered too poor to pay their own health care bills. That number is growing rapidly. In fact, a cottage industry has sprung up to advise middle-income Americans seeking to hide assets legally so that they, too, can be considered poor. This way, Medicaid can pay for their nursing home care. Public assistance for health care in 1993 amounted to $123 billion, more than double the amount spent on medical aid to the poor only five years earlier. In 1993, the government spent almost $14,000 on health care for each "poor" family in the U.S.

Government's increasing involvement in the health care system has led to highly regulated markets dominated by bureaucratic institutions. Unless the very structure of our health care system is changed, it is inevitable that some government or insurance industry bureaucrat, appointed by some politician, will eventually decide which treatments should be given and how much money should be spent to help which individual patients. Ultimately, such bureaucrats will decide whose life is saved and whose is not. Those are very difficult and personal decisions, best left to the individuals whose lives are at stake and their families.

The Solution

Two basic institutional changes are needed to correct the mistakes that have been made in structuring our nation's health care system: empowering patients, and creating competitive markets.

Empowering Patients

After decades of taking health care responsibilities away from individuals, proposals to re-empower patients are beginning to receive a fair hearing. Most of the arguments against "patient power" are variations on a single notion: that individuals are not smart enough or knowledgeable enough to make wise decisions. However, this argument could just as easily be used in every other area. With respect to almost any decision we make, someone else is always smarter or more knowledgeable than we are.

If the case for freedom rested on the assumption that free individuals always make perfect decisions, we would have discarded liberty, and democracy, long ago. The case for empowering patients rests on a different assumption: No one cares more about us than we do.

Creating Competitive Markets

The case for preferring competitive markets over regulated ones is equally persuasive. In regulated markets dominated by bureaucratic institutions, the interests of individuals frequently conflict. One person's gain is another's loss. More for me means less for you, and vice versa.

Quite a different result emerges in competitive markets with clearly defined property rights and freedom of choice. In that environment, you and I cannot pursue our own interests (for the most part) without creating benefits for others. Similarly, others rarely can pursue their interests without creating benefits for us.

In a regulated health care market, such as the one we have today, consumers (patients) are spending other people's money. Most of the decisions are made by insurance companies, employers, and people other than patients themselves. In a competitive, free-market health care system, patients would spend their own money and make most of their own health care decisions.

So how do we get from here to there?

Medical Savings Accounts

As was noted earlier, one of the main complaints about our current health care system is that costs are too high. A key reason for this is that consumers in the health care system—patients—are spending someone else's money. The obvious solution, then, is to change the institutional arrangements so that, to the greatest extent possible, individuals are spending their own money on health care. That can be done through medical savings accounts (MSAs).

A simple change in the tax law (making MSA funds as tax-free as insurance benefits currently are) would encourage employers to establish tax-free MSAs for their employees. Employees would own their MSAs, just as they currently own their individual retirement accounts (IRAs). Like IRAs, MSAs would earn tax-free interest. Employers would get a tax deduction for the funds they contribute to their employees' accounts, just as they now get a deduction for the health insurance premiums they pay.

Used in combination with high-deductible catastrophic health insurance plans, MSAs offer a potent solution to the current health care system's fatal flaw: the reliance on third-party payment for care. With MSAs, major medical expenses would continue to be covered by insurance, but the vast majority of a family's day-to-day medical expenses would be paid out of MSA funds. Individuals would become more cost-conscious in their health care spending, and they would have the financial wherewithal to make most of their own health care decisions. Because most small and routine health care expenses would never go through the insurance claims process, vast amounts of paperwork would be eliminated, resulting in substantial cost savings.

If insurance no longer covered small medical expenses and routine care, would individuals be tempted to ignore necessary doctor visits and other preventive measures in an effort to save money in their MSAs? Early experiments with medical savings accounts suggest that the answer is "no."

In 1993, Golden Rule Insurance Company of Indianapolis established medical savings accounts for its employees. The company discovered that its relatively low-income employees used their MSA funds to pay for the routine exams and doctor visits that they had previously avoided. With their medical savings accounts, employees had the money available to pay for those visits. Without their MSAs, employees could not afford such care because they could not pay the $500 deductible that most policies require before insurance coverage kicks in.

Major Medical Emergencies

Medical savings accounts work best when paired with catastrophic health insurance to cover major medical emergencies. Ideally, this insurance would be purchased by the individual employee, from the money in his or her medical savings account. Moving away from employer-provided health insurance would make it easier for employees to change jobs or withstand periods of unemployment, because their health insurance coverage would not be interrupted.

Also ideally, the catastrophic health insurance purchased by individual employees would operate more like traditional insurance, paying a pre-established, fixed amount for an illness, or a fixed amount per year in the case of an ongoing illness such as cancer. In the event of a major medical problem, the insurance would pay the agreed-upon sum; the patient and family, in consultation with their doctors, would strive to obtain the most cost-effective treatment for the illness.

Patient Power: The "Bottom Line"

A conventional catastrophic health insurance policy with a $3,000 deductible carries an annual premium cost of about $1,500 for a family of four. With a medical savings account of $4,500 (the average amount spent in 1991 on health care by employers and employees in the U.S.), employees could easily purchase their own health insurance policy and still have $3,000 in their MSAs for smaller expenses. Better still, if catastrophic health insurance took the form of real insurance, annual premiums would be even lower, and more money would be available in MSAs for routine expenses.

In either case, an individual's catastrophic health insurance policy should be automatically renewable at the average prevailing rates paid by persons in the same age-sex group, regardless of changes in the person's health, so long as the person stayed in the insurance system. This requirement would protect individuals against one of their greatest fears: becoming uninsured because of illness or unemployment.

The combination of medical savings accounts and catastrophic insurance would end the justification for employer-paid health plans. Health insurance policies would be under the control of individuals, and the policies would continue to provide coverage as the employee moved from one job to another. During periods of unemployment, individuals would use their MSAs to pay for catastrophic health insurance premiums.

Insuring the Elderly and Poor

With private retirement accounts and growing medical savings accounts, the elderly eventually will have sufficient funds to take care of their own health care expenses. However, in the interim, they should be allowed to use a fixed payment from government to purchase either Medicare or a private insurance alternative that might include medical savings accounts. Giving the elderly several such options would inject competition into this segment of the health care system.

Similarly, private social security and medical savings accounts would give most of the poor both the means and the incentive to provide for their own health care. The only group that would fall through the cracks would be those who were unemployed for an extended period of time—a relatively small portion of the population. Government programs could reimburse health care providers for medical services provided to the unemployed when they have exhausted their medical savings accounts and have no other means of payment.

Overcoming the Obstacles

In August 1996, Congress passed and the president signed a health care reform bill that allowed for the creation of a limited experiment with medical savings accounts. Still, countless obstacles stand in the way of proposals that would further empower patients to make their own health care decisions. For one, government still dominates the field. In effect, it tells the elderly that it will take care of the bulk of their health care spending. It has done the same for the poor.

Just as reform of the Social Security system must aim at providing individuals with control over their own retirements, so too must reform of the health care system aim at returning to individuals control over their health care decisions. To the greatest extent possible, individuals should have the resources in their own hands to make their own choices regarding health care. That is the key to the successful operation of the market in a health care system.

The Benefits of Patient Power

Once individuals begin using their own money for health care, a number of positive changes will occur. First, intense competitive pressures will be brought to bear on the health care system. That will tend to improve the quality of health care while lowering its cost. (Those who question whether medical savings accounts can encourage cost-conscious health care shopping, and thus result in significant savings, may find the letter reprinted on page 59 instructive.)

Second, individuals will take more responsibility for their own health and the health care they need. Those individuals who choose a healthy lifestyle (and those who are fortunate enough to avoid ongoing illness) will build up significant financial reserves to add to their retirement accounts or to pay for their health care during retirement.

The savings that can be achieved when individuals control their own health care spending will bolster economic growth and eventually relieve taxpayers of many of Medicare and Medicaid's future burdens. And like the privatization of Social Security, patient power would produce numerous incentives to make legitimate work more attractive than ever before. Under the plan envisioned here, a person with no income may still receive Medicaid—but that person cannot accumulate tax-free funds in a medical savings account. As the accounts of those who work (and remain healthy) grow, those who don't work, or who earn their income illegally, will find that they lose out on the ability to generate savings and wealth. The failure to engage in legitimate, productive work would be reflected clearly and directly in an individual's inability to improve his or her financial well-being.

It is difficult to provide a reliable estimate of the savings that could be expected from a health care system that maximizes the use of market forces and individual incentives. Goodman and Musgrave conservatively estimate savings between $150 and $200 billion a year. However, MSA experiments suggest gains will be even greater. A study reported in the Autumn 1995 issue of the *American Compensation Association Journal* compared the cost of seventeen MSA plans with traditional insurance. In the case of individual policies, the study found average savings of 34 percent over traditional insurance. For family policies, the study found average savings of 54 percent over traditional insurance. Based on those preliminary studies, and on the efficiencies noted in other fields, we can estimate that the widespread use of MSAs is likely to reduce health care costs by 30 to 50 percent. That would produce savings of anywhere from $300 to $500 billion a year. On a per-worker basis, the average savings would be between $2,500 and $4,000 per year.

The potential savings from an efficient health care system are so overwhelming that they easily assure that funds are available to provide all employees with medical savings accounts of $3,000 a year. With these funds, all employees could pay for catastrophic insurance as well as minor medical expenses. Assuming that catastrophic insurance and routine medical expenses average close to $1,500 a year, the lowest-paid worker could have $1,500 a year growing and earning interest in his or her medical savings account.

Those dollars would represent pure savings. Assuming that $1,500 is allowed to accumulate (earning 6 percent a year), the lowest-paid worker would have over $475,000 in a medical savings account upon retirement. Those unspent funds are in addition to the $380,000 that would have accumulated in the worker's private retirement account. All told, the lowest-paid worker would have roughly $855,000 in total assets from just these two public policy changes. Moreover, that worker would have fully paid all of his or her lifetime medical expenses.

The potential gains for most workers would be even greater than for the lowest-paid worker. For 80 percent of all workers, who currently have health insurance, total medical expenses currently amount to between $6,000 and $10,000 a year (including both out-of-pocket expenses and their employers' cost of insurance). For those workers, this new approach to health care would mean saving up to $5,000 a year.

By giving the working poor the means to pay their own medical expenses, these reforms would significantly reduce the need for Medicaid. And, as time passes and funds build up in MSAs and retirement accounts, our health care reforms eventually will reduce the need for Medicare to assist the elderly.

Moving from the current health care system to one characterized by free markets, incentives, and individual responsibility clearly would provide a major boost to creating a nation of millionaires. Moreover, by providing catastrophic insurance for all, the system would assure that a worker's savings would not be wiped out by medical emergencies. For many, the peace of mind associated with such security could itself be worth a million dollars.

Economic Impact on Lowest-Paid Worker: Empowering Patients			
Annual Income at Age 17	$8,840	Annual Income at Age 67	$23,800
Retirement Account at Age 17	$908	Retirement Account at Age 67	$380,000
Medical Savings Account at Age 17	$1,541	Medical Savings Account at Age 67	$475,000

The table above reflects the impact of health care reform, in the form of medical savings accounts, on a 17-year-old worker making $4.25 an hour. The worker's annual income and retirement account are unaffected by this reform, but a new asset is added to the table: the monies that will accumulate in the worker's medical savings account. The graph on the following page shows how the MSA increases the worker's total retirement assets over time.

Retirement Assets of Lowest-Paid Worker:
Medical Savings Accounts

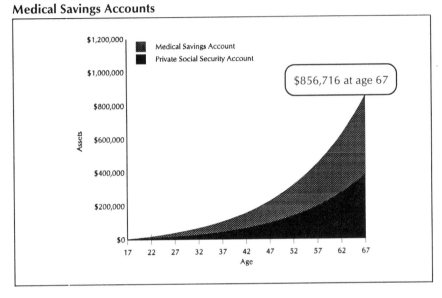

Golden Rule

TO: Pat Rooney
FROM: Shelli Johnson
RE: MSA savings   June 1, 1994

Pursuant to our conversation last week, I am providing you with the details of the experience I had with "shopping around" for a better price on medical care.

After having been told by my primary care physician that I needed to have a couple of tests run at a hospital, I explained to him about my medical savings account and inquired about the cost of the tests. The doctor was uncertain but had his nurses call the local hospital and I was given the following approximate costs:

                 Test 1 — $250.00

                 Test 2 — $295.00

Reading of Test 1 — $120.00

Reading of Test 2 — $120.00

                      $785.00

The grand total of the tests and readings was $785.00. I thought that was way too much, so I asked the doctor to hold off on scheduling the tests until I had time to shop around.

I called several hospitals and was given a wide range of costs. Finally, I found one that was almost too good to be true. St. Vincent's did both tests and readings for a grand total of $114.00! That's a savings of $671.00.

Pat, I know if I had not had a medical savings account, I would never have even thought to ask about the cost of the tests, not to mention thinking of shopping around for a better price.

Source: Golden Rule Insurance Company. Reprinted with permission.

PART THREE

*Cutting the Cost of
Government*

Chapter 5

PRIVATE EDUCATION COSTS LESS?

Nowhere is the influence of government more pronounced than in education. Milton Friedman has described the U.S. education system as a prime example of socialism at work. In the U.S., government owns and controls 88 percent of the production of elementary and secondary education. Not surprisingly, the quality of public education is dismal in all but the wealthiest suburban communities. Moreover, studies indicate that, even where public schools do manage to teach children basic skills, they do so every bit as inefficiently as other government endeavors.

Public versus Private Schools

In 1992, I completed a comprehensive study of the costs of public versus private education in the Chicago area. Two years later, a similar study of Milwaukee-area schools was produced by the city's Public Policy Forum. Unlike earlier research, these studies analyzed school budgets in great detail. Expenditures for teacher salaries, special education, and other categories were analyzed to ensure that the comparisons were valid. The studies reached similar conclusions: Private schools educate children for roughly half the cost of the public school system. Even after allowing for differences in teacher salaries, private school costs were still 25 percent below public school costs.

Those whose living depends on the public school system are understandably defensive about both the quality and the efficiency of their institutions. They contend that their field is an exception to the rule that government-run operations tend to be highly inefficient. They insist that they are as efficient as they possibly can be, blaming the poor quality of education on lazy students, uncaring families, or stingy taxpayers.

In a sense, those who defend public education have a point. Given the monopoly framework in which they operate, they may well be doing as fine a job as can be done. But it is the education system—not its customers—that is at fault. Economists have long recognized that those who operate as monopolists behave differently than do those who operate in a competitive environment. Monopolists seldom, if ever, develop the efficiencies produced in a dynamic, competitive system.

How is it possible for public schools to be almost 50 percent less efficient than private schools? Part of the answer is administration. Public schools are famous—or infamous—for piling on levels of administrators. Some systems include separate vice principals for curriculum, for the building, and for students. Vice principals often have secretaries; they report to the principal, who may in turn report to a superintendent, each of whom also has a secretary. Private schools seldom have more than one administrator—and that administrator often doubles as a teacher.

When public school teachers attend orientation sessions, they are weighed down with pounds of papers detailing school procedures. Rules for behavior, discipline, confrontation management, and every imaginable situation are spelled out in great detail. In most private schools, there is one overriding rule: A student who acts like a jerk will be treated like one. Paper is too valuable to waste on detailed policies and procedures. If additional rules are necessary, they are discussed orally, and if teachers believe they are important enough, they write them down.

In addition to the obvious cost savings in a market-oriented education system, there are more subtle economies. In a suburban Chicago school district, a transportation consultant explained how a ten-minute change to the school's bus schedule would save the district $900,000 a year in transportation costs. One principal became highly indignant that anyone would place a dollar value on the time spent in school by the district's students. He succeeded in keeping the schedule the way it was.

A few weeks later, the transportation consultant discovered the real reason the bus schedule wasn't changed. The principal was working a second job that would have been threatened by the change. In a system characterized by market pressures, such a decision would have been far less possible. In the government-run system, such decisions are far more common than most people realize.

Public school system administrators today can count on a constant flow of "customers" and taxpayer money, almost regardless of their performance. Private schools, by contrast, operate as businesses in the real world. They face the prospect of going out of business if they fail to provide a superior product at the lowest possible cost. Nothing stimulates efficiency more than the need to survive.

The Worldwide Choice Revolution

Worldwide, more and more people are recognizing that government-run education systems waste scarce resources that could be put to better use. Chile, Poland, Sweden, and Russia are among the countries that now issue the equivalent of education vouchers to families with children. The vouchers represent anywhere from 50 to 100 percent of the cost of a public education. The families are free to use the vouchers at a school of their choice, which introduces competition into the education system.

The education establishment in the United States fully recognizes the attractiveness of choice in education. It counters by promoting choice among only public schools—a proposal not unlike giving individuals their choice of deck chairs on the Titanic. As the excessive costs of public education become apparent to a sufficient number of taxpayers, the education monopoly will be broken.

My study of the impact of privatizing education in Chicago showed that the savings to taxpayers would be sufficient to eliminate more than 90 percent of the property taxes devoted to education. Moreover, such a study may significantly underestimate the true savings. In many states, pension funds for state employees (including teachers) have not been fully funded. Those underfunded pensions represent a considerable tax liability for future taxpayers and further add to the true costs of public education.

Introducing more competition into education would do more than ease the burden on taxpayers; it would revolutionize the education process. Many teachers are so burned-out from the present system that their main focus is on vacation or retirement. A revitalized, competitive system would provide new challenges for teachers, students, *and* parents as they strive for excellence together.

The first stage of the transition from public to private education has already begun. Public authorities have begun to contract with private businesses to administer their education systems. While private management of school systems can improve the quality of education and lower costs somewhat, such limited privatization is likely to tap only a small portion of the potential of a true free-market education system. As the operation of private schools shows, the benefits from localized, independent schools can far exceed anything that could be achieved merely by transferring a massive, publicly run bureaucracy into the hands of one that is massive but privately run. The education system will not experience the full benefits of privatization so long as it has a monopoly over its customers.

The Voucher Solution

In order to achieve the maximum savings from a true market system, power must be placed in the hands of individual customers, not bureaucrats. The most effective means of accomplishing this is to provide parents with a voucher for the cost of a public education. Parents would use the voucher to pay for tuition at the school of their choice.

To give public schools an opportunity to compete with private schools on a more even footing, each public school should be given complete control over its curriculum, the hiring and firing of teachers, and the dismissal of students for disciplinary reasons. Dismissed students could then use their voucher at a school specializing in educating students with disciplinary problems. Competition among those special disciplinary schools would help to produce effective programs for treating these students and returning them to conventional schools.

The value of the vouchers could be set at anywhere from 50 to 100 percent of the cost of a public education, depending on how much money taxpayers decided to devote to education. Various studies suggest that there is no significant relationship between the amount of money spent on education and the quality of the education. Hence, to maximize efficiency, it would be appropriate to set the value of the vouchers at somewhere between 50 and 75 percent of the cost of a public education. During the transition period, vouchers that are used at public schools might be redeemed at 100 percent of the cost of a public education. Doing so would continue to give the less-efficient public sector the "cushion" it is likely to need to adjust to market pressures.

Eventually, taxpayers might question the wisdom of subsidizing this inefficiency. Once that issue is addressed, all educational costs could be reduced. It is interesting that those countries that have had the most experience with government-run entities seem to have the least concern for their survival. In Russia, the public schools are not given any "cushion" to allow them to continue to operate less efficiently than private schools; education vouchers, regardless of where they are spent, are worth 100 percent of the cost of a public education.

The combination of incentives and competitive pressures would force education to be as efficient as other private businesses. Inefficient schools that failed to produce a high-quality product would lose students. If the schools failed to adjust, they would go out of business. Efficient schools producing a high-quality education would prosper. As they attracted more students and more voucher funds, they would be able to reward their teachers and administrators with higher pay. As in any other business, teachers and administrators who performed best would tend to receive the highest compensation. The less competent would seek employment in other fields.

In the process, not only would the quality of education improve, but taxpayers would eventually save 25 to 50 percent of the amount spent on education. In 1995, government at all levels in the U.S. spent roughly $275 billion on elementary and secondary education. Privatizing education holds the potential to save $70 to $140 billion a year.

Using the midpoint of this range means that privatizing education would save over $100 billion a year—more than $800 a year for each worker. Moreover, under the proposed system of private social security, the savings would mean an extra $80 a year in each worker's retirement account. Over a lifetime, the lowest-paid worker's retirement assets would increase by about $35,000. This may not seem like much compared to the first two reforms, but any millionaire will tell you that every little bit counts! Also, the savings would not merely create more millionaires, but better-educated ones as well.

Economic Impact on Lowest-Paid Worker: Private Education			
Annual Income at Age 17	+$800	Annual Income at Age 67	+$2,100
Retirement Account at Age 17	+$80	Retirement Account at Age 67	+$35,000

Annual Income of Lowest-Paid Worker:
Wage Plus Savings from Private Education

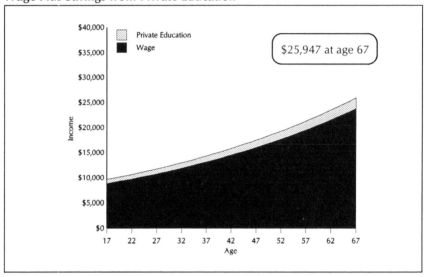

Retirement Assets of Lowest-Paid Worker:
Private Education

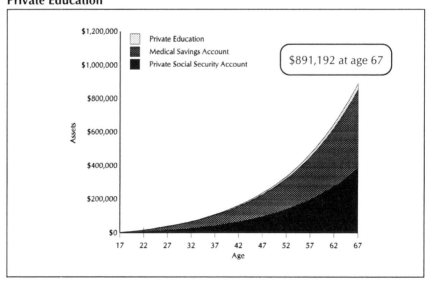

Chapter 6

REGULATION AS TAXATION

In 1988, before the recent explosion in government regulation, a federal government agency tried to estimate the amount of time it took to complete government forms. The answer: roughly five billion hours a year! That's the equivalent of 2.5 million people working full-time all year long just to do government paperwork.

And completing forms is only one part of the cost of government regulations. When 2.5 million people are engaged in paperwork instead of producing something useful, everyone is worse off. Even those whose job includes filling out forms will find that their living standard is lower than it would have been. Had these people been engaged in productive work, everyone would enjoy more output.

Economists place government regulations into several categories. Economic regulations attempt to protect people from the potential harsh consequences of a competitive, free-market system. Social regulations address health and safety. Process regulations enforce those activities that are necessary to comply with government mandates.

Economic regulations, which include trade barriers, antitrust laws, and minimum-wage laws, help some people while hurting others. They give rise to transfer costs, imposed by one group on another. When limits are placed on importing things such as sugar, clothing, or automobiles, for example, consumers pay higher prices; the benefits are transferred to sugar producers, textile manufacturers, auto makers, and their employees. On balance, economic research shows that the rewards to specific groups from economic regulations tend to be overwhelmed by the penalties to consumers.

Social regulations attempt to protect the health and safety of the population. They include environmental laws, food and drug protection, and workplace safety requirements. Studies of the benefits and costs from social regulation have found that benefits seldom exceed or even equal costs. In many areas, social regulations have been found to be highly ineffective. The Occupational Safety and Health Administration (OSHA), for example, appears to have had no significant impact on workplace accident rates, worker safety, or illness. The Food and Drug Administration (FDA) has been accused of preventing the use of life-saving drugs, while the Consumer Product Safety Commission appears to have had no significant impact on product safety. And the list goes on.

The most obvious and most costly example of process regulation is complying with the tax codes. In 1995, the IRS estimated that businesses and individuals spent just over five billion hours a year in tax-related paperwork alone. That is the equivalent of 2.5 million people—more than serve in the armed forces—working full time just to comply with tax laws. (The reader may recall from the opening of this chapter that in 1988—just seven years earlier—*all* forms of government paperwork combined required this much effort.)

The justification for the government's huge regulatory system stems from a belief that there are certain areas where the free market, left to its own, has failed to protect people. However, economists have begun to analyze this issue. Recent literature strongly suggests that what has been viewed as a failure of markets to produce desirable outcomes is actually a failure of the legal system to protect property rights. For example, as will be discussed in the following chapter, air and water pollution often goes unaddressed because there is no clear property right to the air or water. Laws that define more clearly the rights people have to clean air and clean water have the potential for addressing environmental concerns far more efficiently and effectively than the present tangle of extensive regulation.

The most comprehensive and respected study of the direct costs of government regulation was conducted by Professor Thomas Hopkins at the Rochester Institute of Technology. His figures, including the transfer costs discussed earlier, show that regulations cost the economy roughly $650 billion a year—approximately $6,000 per worker each year. Without the transfers, the cost per worker is $5,333 per year.

Hopkins' study is the best available analysis of the cost of government regulation, but it touches only the tip of the iceberg. Hopkins is purposely conservative in his estimates. He does not include the cost of regulation to government, nor does he include the cost of complying with state and local regulations. Also, if no reliable study exists to document the cost of complying with a given regulation, Hopkins assumes that the cost is zero. From a practical standpoint, the true cost of government regulations may be double Hopkins' figure.

Do Benefits Outweigh Costs?

Of course, government regulations produce benefits, as well as costs. Unfortunately, the benefits tend to be relatively small. The substantial efficiency gains that followed deregulation of the transportation industry suggest that the cost of government regulation far exceeds the benefits. That is why those who favor government regulations strongly oppose requiring that those regulations be subjected to cost/benefit analysis.

In an as-yet unpublished paper, economist William Laffer attempts to measure the net costs of regulations after allowing for benefits. Laffer's estimate of net costs is $6,000 per year, and this does not include environmental costs, legal costs, and indirect costs (all of which are considered in the following chapters).

The cost of regulation is clearly substantial. Even if the lower-end estimate is used, regulations cost the economy a substantial amount each year. Moreover, the burden of these regulations falls hardest on those with low and moderate incomes. Regulations may have reduced household incomes in the U.S. by an average of $6,000 a year. That amount may not seem particularly important to a family whose annual income is $100,000. Such wealthy families might even praise the regulations that generated those costs, and tell others they would like to see more of such policies. But those whose annual household incomes are closer to $10,000 will find that regulations require them to sacrifice income that could have provided their families with more adequate meals, better health care, or improved education. The ability to purchase such things may affect that family more positively than any government regulation.

This does not mean that government regulation is necessarily bad. But those who favor regulation have an obligation to make sure that the regulation is as efficient as possible at accomplishing its objective. This has not been the case. As a result, the typical household is probably close to $6,000 a year poorer than it would have been without the direct adverse effect of inappropriate government regulations.

The Benefits of Regulatory Reform

On a more positive note, regulatory reform has the potential to add roughly $6,000 of income to the average household each year. The way to accomplish this is to replace the present bureaucratic approach to regulation with an approach that maximizes the use of competitive, free-market forces.

The first logical step in such an approach would be to estimate the potential costs and benefits to different groups from the present regulatory regime. An independent commission, such as the General Services Administration or the General Accounting Office, could be used to provide those estimates. That commission could assess the risks associated with particular events, such as driving an auto without certain safety devices. The commission would then evaluate those risks alongside all others. Once the risks were listed, the commission would attempt to estimate the costs associated with abating those risks in the most efficient way possible.

This process would lead those in charge of the regulatory system to discover that the most cost-effective way to reduce risks will utilize competitive, free-market pressures. The commission would consider not only economic and social regulations, but also process regulations. In doing so it would find, as others have found, that replacing the current income tax with a simple flat tax is likely to save over $200 billion a year.

Once it is presented with these studies, Congress will be in a better position to evaluate the costs and benefits of regulations in different areas. This approach would help efficiently reduce the risks faced by individuals. Also, highlighting the costs of process regulations versus their benefits should help encourage efficiency in government operations.

It is difficult to place a precise figure on the direct gains from sound regulatory reform. At the lower end of the range is Hopkins' figure, which estimates that the cost of regulation is roughly $5,300 per worker. At the other end is Laffer's estimate, showing $6,000 per worker *after* allowing for benefits. Given the inefficiencies that have been discovered whenever bureaucracies and regulations are involved, it is likely that Laffer's figure comes closer to measuring the true costs that regulations impose on the economy.

Rather than accept those figures completely, we'll assume very conservatively that broad regulatory reform would produce gains equivalent to $3,000 per worker—just half the Laffer estimate. Just as the lowest-paid worker's wage is expected to increase by 2 percent a year, the same would be true for the savings from regulatory reform. Over the lifetime of our 17-year-old worker, this additional $3,000 in income would increase to $8,075 by age 67. By that time, the additional income from regulatory reform will have boosted the worker's retirement account by roughly $129,000. That additional savings would leave the lowest-paid worker with just over a million dollars in assets upon retirement. Although our objective has been reached, there is still more to come.

Economic Impact on Lowest-Paid Worker: Regulatory Reform			
Annual Income at Age 17	+$3,000	Annual Income at Age 67	+$8,075
Retirement Account at Age 17	+$308	Retirement Account at Age 67	+$129,000

Annual Income of Lowest-Paid Worker:
Wage Plus Savings from Reforms

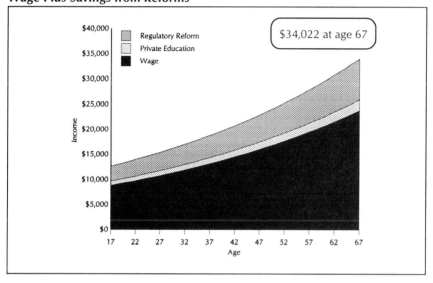

Retirement Assets of Lowest-Paid Worker:
Regulatory Reform

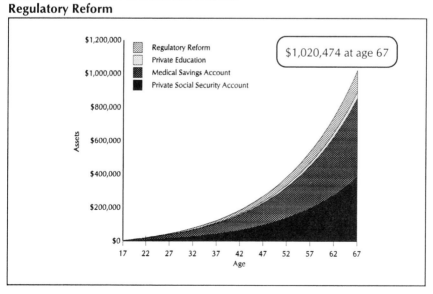

Chapter 7

PRICING
THE ENVIRONMENT

For most people, protecting the environment is a high priority. The more money people have, the greater their concern. Millionaires (or those who have wealthy parents) tend to be more concerned about environmental quality than poor people are. The reason is simple. The poor have many more immediate problems than clean air and clean water. It is difficult to become too worked up over global warming if you're wondering how to pay your heating bill.

The wealthy are different. They not only have more money, but since all their immediate wants are taken care of, they want a better quality of life. No matter how much money people have, they breathe the same air and swim in the same rivers, lakes, and oceans as others. Once a person's immediate surroundings are as comfortable as possible, the next logical step is to extend that comfort to the rest of the world. If everyone is going to become a millionaire, then everyone will eventually face the problems that millionaires face. Improving the environment is one of them.

There are a host of controversies surrounding environmental problems and what to do about them. Wading through the issues can be mind-boggling even if you are an environmental scientist. For non-experts, the hysteria surrounding claims and counter-claims regarding the environment can be extremely frustrating.

Fortunately, some basic guidelines can help anyone understand and deal intelligently with environmental issues.

- ✔ View environmental quality as a product.
- ✔ Determine the true value of environmental quality.
- ✔ Organize institutions to produce environmental quality at the least possible cost.

Choosing Environmental Protection

The first point is to recognize that environmental quality must be viewed as another good or product. Just as people want more and better food, clothing, shelter, and entertainment, they want more and better environmental quality. Environmental quality is not necessarily more or less important than other things. But if we want more of it, we must give up something else. Every time we place limits on toxins or pollutants that enter the air or water, it means that we will get less of other things. The first key to sound policy is to make certain that we understand those tradeoffs.

As basic as that point is, it is often ignored. Some have tried to hide the costs of improving environmental quality by referring to such expenditures as *investments* in the future. While efforts to improve the environment may indeed be investments in the future, those investments involve costs here and now. It is deceitful to focus on benefits while ignoring the costs—and it leads to bad decision-making.

Some environmental activists behave as if improving the environment should take precedence over all else. But surely some things are more important. Food, health care, clothing, and shelter are all more immediate concerns for most people than environmental issues. It makes no sense to abandon the necessities of life in order to preserve life.

At times, seemingly reasonable ideas for improving the environment conflict with reality. In 1958 Congress passed the Delaney Clause, which forbids the presence in food of any chemical that causes cancer. That certainly seems reasonable. After all, who in their right mind would favor adding carcinogenic chemicals to food? But as is often the case, something that seems straightforward simply is not.

A study of the causes of death in the U.S. shows that 20 percent of Americans die from cancer. Of that 20 percent, 75 percent die from cancer that results from the way people choose to live their lives. Three-quarters of all cancer deaths result from such lifestyle choices as smoking, alcohol abuse, poor eating habits, and irresponsible sexual behavior. Of the remaining cancer deaths, food additives are believed to account for less than 1 percent. Put another way: Lifestyle choices account for 150,000 deaths from cancer out of each 1 million people; deaths from food additives account for fewer than 2,000 deaths out of each million.

And even the two thousand deaths per million may overstate the danger. Pesticides and preservatives reduce spoilage rates for food. This, in turn, reduces the risk of food poisoning and makes food considerably less expensive. Both of these results lower death rates much more than pesticides and food additives could possibly raise them. If banning cancer-causing food additives caused the price of food to rise by 10 or 20 percent, the immediate adverse effects in terms of malnutrition would far outweigh the benefit of delaying the deaths of two thousand people out of a million.

It's also worth noting that foods contain *natural* carcinogens. Plants develop their own pesticides to protect themselves from insects and fungus. The Delaney Clause led to the banning of some food additives, yet permitted far higher concentrations of cancer-causing elements that occur naturally. That irony is among the factors that led Congress to repeal the Delaney Clause in 1996.

Environmental issues are seldom as simple as banning all pollutants. That is why environmental quality must be viewed as another product. We can make wise choices about how clean the environment should be only if we clearly understand the costs and benefits.

The Value of Environmental Protection

It is not enough to recognize that environmental quality is a product. The next step is to understand the true *value* of that product. As the cancer-causing food additives scenario shows, a clear improvement in environmental quality can be difficult to realize. It becomes even more complicated as individuals and groups use environmental issues to promote their own agendas. Extremists in the environmental movement often use apocalyptic forecasts to scare people into placing an unrealistically high value on their own environmental product.

At various times these impending disasters have included over-population, mass starvation, depletion of the Earth's resources, nuclear disaster, the coming of a new ice age, global warming, and holes in the ozone layer. The threat of imminent environmental disaster has become a popular ploy of even mainstream environmentalists. To those who buy into such scare tactics, nothing less than the preservation of the world is at stake. Saving the world is certainly a worthy goal. But it should come as no surprise that the matter is far more complicated than it first appears.

Eco-Scam, by Ronald Bailey, carefully explores the environmental scares of the past few decades. The book recalls the population explosion, starvation, and disease that were predicted to hit the United States by the early 1980s. It goes on to describe the nuclear holocaust that was supposed to annihilate mankind. Then, it discusses the coming ice age, a popular fear in the 1970s, and the more recent global warming scare.

All of those dire predictions have at least one thing in common: They are impossible to disprove. Try as we might, we cannot prove that something will not happen, except by waiting (which can take forever). In the meantime, however, we can use common sense to help us evaluate predictions of environmental doom.

In his book, *Earth in the Balance*, Vice President Al Gore strongly implies that 98 percent of the scientific community agrees that global warming is a serious threat. However, a recent survey of climatologists— scientists who work in the field of climate research—found that only 17 percent considered global warming a real threat.

Interestingly, at least two of the world's leading climate scientists contend that the build-up of CO_2 and global warming are *good* things. They note that warmer temperatures and higher levels of CO_2 tend to be helpful to life, while cold is life-threatening. Other scientists note that there have been seventeen climate cycles in the past three million years, with ice ages lasting roughly 100,000 years interrupted by warm periods lasting roughly 10,000 years. Since the current warm period is about 13,000 years old, some feel that the next ice age is overdue.

The object here is not to resolve disputes over global warming or any other environmental issue. Rather, it is to show that broad agreement regarding certain environmental issues simply does not exist. And, since correcting major environmental problems may involve a huge expense (assuming they can be corrected), it would be nice to know that our efforts would be productive. And it would be nice to have some reasonable assurance that our efforts were not working *against* what is really needed.

Understanding the Apocalyptics

A bystander in the debate over key environmental issues might wonder why anyone would predict environmental disaster if the scientific evidence were not persuasive. The reasons are as old as man: control and greed.

In evaluating the apocalyptic forecasts, some authors have noticed a curious thing. No matter what the problem, the prophets of doom propose the same four-part solution. First, they demand that a command-and-control system be established whereby some government agency dictates the way people live. Next, they propose major new taxes on all types of activities. Then, the new tax dollars would be used to support government efforts to stave off the threatened catastrophe. Finally, there are demands of a more political nature: redistributing income, achieving social justice, and accomplishing land reform.

The closer one looks at these proposals, the clearer it becomes that the overriding objective is to dictate how people should live their lives, rather than to improve environmental quality. What do redistribution of income or social justice have to do with improving environmental quality?

The political agenda is not so out-of-place as it appears. Many of today's radical environmentalists are recycled 1960s Marxists. Unable to persuade the world to abandon economic freedom for political reasons, they now seek to restrict freedom for environmental reasons. Their environmentalism is little more than a new effort to reach an old, rejected goal.

Of course, not all of the apocalyptic environmentalists are Marxists. Some are economically illiterate. Still others have more in common with the most legendary of greedy capitalists: They want money, and they have learned that bad news sells.

The financial well-being of powerful environmental groups is often tied directly to how important their work seems. The more fear they can generate, the greater their income.

Even scientists have learned that lesson. Environmental groups have a major influence on Congressional appropriations for research. Those scientists whose research shows the most dire implications stand a better chance of receiving government research funds. Those whose research fails to confirm apocalyptic visions of destruction can expect to lose out in the battle for research funds.

To make matters worse, fear sells in the media, too. Print and broadcast journalists are far more likely to publicize frightening news than they are to reassure people that they are safe and secure. For that reason, there is a significant bias in media coverage of the debate over environmental policy. Hidden agendas, greed, and media bias make evaluating environmental quality exceedingly difficult.

One of the best reviews of the evidence concerning environmental problems can be found in *Eco-Sanity: A Common-Sense Guide to Environmentalism*, by Joseph Bast, Peter Hill, and Richard Rue. The authors are environmentalists who have sifted through the scientific evidence on several key environmental issues. Among their important conclusions: In the United States, the environment is cleaner today than at any time in the past half-century; the environment is safer than at any time in recorded history; cancer rates are falling, not rising; and predictions of impending global disasters are untrue.

Cutting the Cost of Environmental Protection

One reason environmental quality is improving is that a lot of money is being spent on this effort. Each year, well over $100 billion—over $1,000 per worker—is spent to protect the environment. While this spending has contributed to a cleaner environment, it has done so at a significant cost in terms of tax dollars, lost jobs, slower technological advancement, and diminished personal liberties. Environmental issues are often approached in a way that offers few benefits for the money spent.

This leads to the third point for addressing environmental concerns: Institutions should be organized in such a way as to produce the greatest environmental quality at the least possible cost. Institutions should ensure that individuals derive personal gain for environmentally good behavior and bear personal cost for environmentally bad behavior. Institutions organized in this way would encourage individuals to use resources as efficiently as possible while avoiding the pollution of other people's property. This, in turn, would produce environmental improvement *and* enhance living standards. The only system that can accomplish this is the free-market, private-property system.

In a free-market system, prices reflect the value that buyers place on products, as well as the costs associated with providing those products. Without prices, we cannot know how much a product is worth to people or what it costs to produce it. And without this information, it is impossible to make efficient use of resources.

Like prices, property rights are essential to the proper functioning of a free-market system. The role of property rights is to ensure that individuals who own property will benefit from it. When property is improved and used wisely, owners enjoy a financial gain and are better off. If there is any damage to the property, or if it is squandered, the owners suffer a loss and are worse off.

A free-market system with well-defined property rights provides individuals with strong incentives to do the right things: to produce the products people want with the most efficient combination of resources and, at the same time, to improve and protect the value of all privately owned property. It is the only system that can efficiently and effectively maximize environmental quality.

My suggestion that the free market is the best protector of the environment may surprise some readers. Many Americans have been led to believe that environmental problems are *caused* by the free market and private property owners. But nothing could be further from the truth.

There are two ways to achieve a significant improvement in environmental quality. Both involve free markets and private property rights. The first is to extend free markets and private property rights throughout the economy. Doing so will dramatically increase living standards, which in turn will ensure that money is available to clean the environment. The second is to apply the concepts of free markets and private property specifically to environmental issues.

Economic Growth and the Environment

As living standards rise, so does the quality of the environment. One of the most predictable things about environmental quality is that it tends to improve as incomes rise. The reason for this is obvious. Higher incomes and greater wealth make it financially possible to clean and protect the environment. Until individuals are satisfied with their standard of living, the environment will take a back seat to more pressing concerns. Without a strong and growing economy, the environmental movement withers and dies for lack of interest.

Socialist countries have much to teach the United States in this regard. Growing at roughly one-third the rate of market-oriented democratic countries, socialist countries produced widespread environmental degradation. Their experience strongly suggests that the single greatest threat to the environment comes not from pollutants, but from a failure to boost living standards.

Countries that have not organized their economies around free markets and private property rights generally have not prospered. Without prosperity, they don't have the money to spend on environmental protection. It is ironic that extreme environmentalists seek to change the only economic system capable of providing the environmental improvements they claim to desire.

How Government Hurts the Environment

As the socialist nations have shown, a country that lacks free markets and private property rights will inevitably use resources inefficiently and experience lower living standards. Similarly, a nation that abandons the free market in any part of its economy will produce problems in that area. The United States itself proves this point. In the U.S., most environmental problems developed because we abandoned free markets and property rights, instead applying the socialist system of publicly owned property to things such as air and water.

Why does a socialist system protect the environment so ineffectively? Because socialism relies on top-down commands and controls to accomplish its objectives. In a socialist system, the value of products, including environmental protection, is determined by politics—by the degree of political pressure brought to bear by special interest groups. That is why governments make so many decisions that appear so ridiculous. We should expect nothing more from political decision-making.

Similarly, resources allocated through political processes will be allocated inefficiently. The command-and-control approach precludes the use of vital information on the true cost of the resources involved. Prices change on a daily basis; each day, the most efficient combination of resources for producing anything will change. The market system is the only system able to continuously respond to those changes. Therefore, it is the only system that can utilize resources in the most efficient manner.

Finally, when property is owned by the state, it is really owned by no one. It is in no one's interest to take the time and effort necessary to care for the property. It is only in people's self-interest to spend their time and energy taking care of what they own.

Before the collapse of the Soviet Union, all property there was owned by "the people." In practice, this meant that no one owned anything. When property is owned in common, individuals receive little if any personal benefit from protecting or improving it, and there is seldom any cost to abusing it. Nowhere in the world has the environment been polluted worse than in the countries of the former Soviet Union, where government was responsible for its care.

It is no accident that a similar pattern exists in the United States. The worst polluter has been government. Its lands are among the worst-kept in the country. The Defense Department is notorious for leaving toxic wastes exposed; municipalities are notorious for dumping sewage and trash into rivers, lakes, and oceans. These environmental degradations could occur because no owner could come forward to complain.

England and Scotland offer a stark contrast. In those countries, there are property rights for both sport and commercial fishing. Those rights are valuable, and they are protected. Those who pollute rivers and streams are quickly sued by the owners for destroying their property. Similarly, in Yellowstone River Valley there is a stream that begins and ends on private property. It is one of very few streams in the country that are privately owned. Sportsmen from all over the world pay the stream's owners fees to fish some of the most crystal-clear waters they have ever seen. The owners have a financial incentive to keep the stream pollution-free and well stocked with fish.

When a government agency attempts to improve the environment by identifying thousands of pollutants emitted by hundreds of sources, and then specifying exactly how much of each pollutant can be spewed into the environment by each source, it is using the socialist model to achieve its objectives. When a government agency mandates that a specific type of technology must be used to achieve an environmental goal—that power plants using high-sulfur coal *must* use "scrubbers" to reduce emissions, or that automobile manufacturers *must* produce electric cars to reduce emissions, or that consumers *must* buy reformulated gasoline—it is using the socialist model to achieve its objectives.

Socialism depends on a massive bureaucracy to enforce its top-down regulations. It depends on special interest group politics to determine what pollutant should be controlled, who is a polluter, and what polluters should be required to do to mitigate their pollution. In the end, socialist systems often fall far short of achieving their objectives. In the United States, older, dirtier power plants are treated more leniently than newer, cleaner ones, because of the costs of shutting down the older plants. So older plants are encouraged to continue to pollute; newer, less-polluting plants are less likely to be built. Pollutants and sources that are more politically vulnerable are singled out for control. Those that can avoid becoming a political target continue to pollute.

Market-Based Environmental Protection

The alternative approach to addressing environmental problems is to rely on free markets and private property rights. How can these be applied to the environment?

First, by establishing an independent agency to help determine the likely risks associated with various environmental concerns. Second, by establishing property rights to important resources such as clean air and clean water. And third, by using the free market to determine the most efficient way to solve the problems.

In the first step, an independent agency or committee would assess the risks associated with each environmental problem—everything from global warming to species endangerment to hormone-mimicking chemicals. Those risks would be ranked and compared to other risks so that the public could better appreciate the relative importance of various problems. The committee might also offer rough estimates of the likely cost of lowering the most serious risks. The purpose of the committee would be limited to gathering and releasing information. It would review the credibility of each alleged new threat to the environment and offer a balanced assessment of that risk and the cost associated with correcting it. To avoid personal agendas, the agency should be modeled after the General Accounting Office or General Services Administration. Those agencies are given broad responsibility for identifying waste and inefficiency in government.

The second step—expanding property rights—is obviously tricky. Still, with enough imagination, it can be done. For example, instead of enforcing a government edict that sets pollution limits, the legal system would be directed to recognize each individual's right to clean, healthy air and clean, safe drinking water. Those who pollute the air and water to such an extent that it affects the health or property of others would be held liable for that damage. If some person or group could prove in court that their respiratory problems were the result of pollutants from certain factories, the factories' owners would be liable.

Similarly, establishing fishing rights for commercial companies and sports clubs would give these groups the right to sue polluters who damage the value of the fish. More importantly, the owners of these rights would be constantly on the watch for early signs of pollution, overfishing, or any other act that would endanger the value of their rights.

The third step—utilizing free markets—is also tricky. In the case of promoting clean air, government could use guidelines suggested by the independent committee to determine an acceptable level of pollution within a certain geographic area. It would then issue pollution permits that reflect the maximum amount of pollution to be allowed. Those permits would be auctioned off to the highest bidders and could then be sold and traded.

A pollution permit trading system makes clear to potential polluters in the region that there is a cost to polluting. The more they reduce pollution, the less they would need to spend buying permits. For some firms, reducing emissions would be relatively inexpensive. Those firms would not need the permits, and could easily avoid the cost of purchasing them. Other firms that would face great expense in reducing pollution would find it advantageous to purchase permits. However, the cost of the permits would act as a constant reminder of the extra costs associated with polluting the environment. Such a system is far more efficient than mandating, across-the-board, that all firms reduce emissions by some arbitrarily determined amount.

Polluting firms are not the only ones who would participate in the permit trading. Environmentalists, too, could bid for the permits. If their desire for a clean environment is matched by financial resources, they would buy the pollution permits in order to keep them out of the hands of polluting firms, thereby forcing the firms to cut their emissions.

Over time, as the costs and technology associated with pollution change, and as new environmental problems emerge, environmentalists might choose to sell their permits and use the funds for more pressing problems. The whole idea is to give each individual worker, each firm, and each environmentally conscious person an incentive to use his or her imagination and resources to reduce pollution, while clearly recognizing the costs and benefits that are involved.

If a pollution permit trading system is to function properly, it is critically important that permit owners be given full property rights to them. This means that the permits can be bought and sold in a free market; that courts will uphold the rights conferred by these permits in the future; and that the government agency that issued the permits (or some future political administration) cannot later decide to abandon the program. If one firm buys all the permits, the agency cannot decide to issue new ones to "level the playing field," nor can that firm be told that it must reduce pollution regardless of the permits it holds. In short, once the program is in place, its participants must have protections against future government interventions into the market.

Benefits of Market-Based Environmentalism

The speed at which environmental problems can be solved depends on a careful assessment of risk and the ability to use property rights and market forces to design an efficient, effective solution. Judging from the inefficiencies that are often associated with the socialist model, it is likely that 50 percent of the funds that presently go toward cleaning the environment are wasted. It was noted earlier that the U.S. currently spends more than $100 billion—over $1,000 per worker—on improving the environment. Switching to the free-market, private-property approach thus holds the potential to save $500 for each worker, each year.

Since the rich tend to be more willing to sacrifice for environmental concerns than the poor, creating more millionaires is not only desirable for obvious reasons, but it's very likely the greatest single contribution that could be made toward improving environmental quality. A nation of millionaires would be more likely to demand environmental improvement and would have the financial resources to make that improvement. Their efforts would affect environmental quality not only in the United States, but in other countries as well.

An additional $500 in income for each worker each year (in addition to the reforms mentioned in previous chapters) would raise the annual income of the lowest-paid 17-year-old worker to just over $13,000. Growing at 2 percent a year, the additional income would raise the salary of the lowest-paid worker to over $35,000 after fifty years. The increased income would increase the value of the worker's individual retirement account by just over $21,000. By age 67, the lowest-paid worker would have a retirement account worth roughly $565,000. Along with the $475,000 from the medical savings account balance, the reforms considered up to this point will have left the lowest-paid worker with a retirement portfolio of roughly $1,040,000.

Economic Impact on Lowest-Paid Worker: Free-Market Environmentalism			
Annual Income at Age 17	+$500	Annual Income at Age 67	+$1,346
Retirement Account at Age 17	+$51	Retirement Account at Age 67	+$21,000

Annual Income of Lowest-Paid Worker
Wage Plus Savings from Reforms

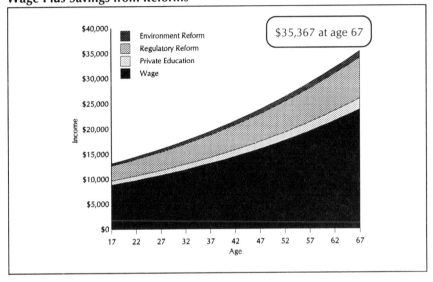

$35,367 at age 67

Legend:
- Environment Reform
- Regulatory Reform
- Private Education
- Wage

Retirement Assets of Lowest-Paid Worker:
Environment Reform

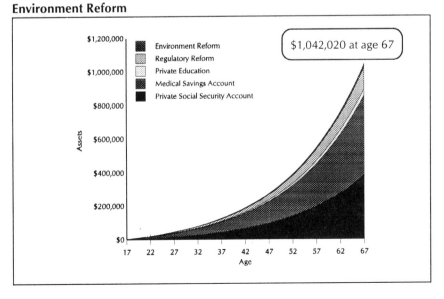

$1,042,020 at age 67

Legend:
- Environment Reform
- Regulatory Reform
- Private Education
- Medical Savings Account
- Private Social Security Account

Chapter 8

THERE OUGHT
TO BE A LAW

One day God discovered that the fence between heaven and hell was two feet into heaven. When He went down to talk it over, the Devil was obviously surprised.

"What in the hell are you doing here?" he asked.

"It seems that the fence between heaven and hell is two feet into heaven," came the reply.

"So what?" asked the Devil.

"So I want it moved, or else," said God.

"Or else what?" asked Satan. "What do you intend to do about it?"

"I'll sue," came the divine reply.

"Oh," said the Devil, "and just where do you expect to get a lawyer?"

The legal system has taken its share of criticism, much of it well deserved. The system suffers from many abuses that have cost Americans greatly, while producing few benefits. The direct waste produced by the U.S. legal system is estimated at $75 billion a year—$625 for each worker, each year.

In addition to this financial waste, the legal system suffers from a clear moral problem. Frivolous suits and a generous system of punitive damage awards have helped make the United States the most litigious society on the face of the Earth. Without proper legal reforms, a nation of millionaires will be a goal out of reach in the U.S. Even if the objective were achieved, many of the millionaires would probably end up suing each other, rather than using their wealth productively.

Before addressing the legal system's shortcomings, however, we should note that no civilized nation could exist without a legal system. Laws are essential to establish and protect the property rights of individuals, to enforce contracts, and to provide a means to punish those whose actions damage the well-being or property of others. Without institutions to perform those functions, society would degenerate into chaos. Little if any productive activity would occur. Hence, a legal system is an essential component of any advanced society. It is indispensable to prosperity.

The Founding Fathers knew the importance of a sound legal system. Through the Constitution, they established a system designed to protect each individual's property, not only from other individuals, but from government itself. They also enshrined in the Bill of Rights an individual's right to a trial by a jury of peers and protection against self-incrimination and cruel and unusual punishment.

Areas of Judicial Abuse

So long as the basic tenets set forth by the Founding Fathers were respected, the legal system worked as it should. However, as society evolved, many of those basic tenets have been eroded or even abandoned. The result often has been a mockery of justice, social unrest, and a situation where victims have more to fear from the legal system than do criminals. The legal system has faltered under such burdens as the erosion of property rights, acquiescence to frivolous lawsuits and punitive damages, and a liberal interpretation of the prohibition against cruel and unusual punishment.

Private Property and Just Compensation

The erosion of property rights represents the most destructive abuse of individual rights. This abuse is well documented in Richard Epstein's book *Takings: Private Property and the Power of Eminent Domain*. He traces the importance of protecting property, from common law foundations to the Fifth Amendment. That amendment's "takings clause" plainly states "nor shall private property be taken for public use, without just compensation." While early Supreme Court decisions upheld the idea that government could take private property only for "public use" and the "purpose of the general welfare," and only then with "just compensation," subsequent rulings eroded those protections. Public use became any use the legislature decided was public; the general welfare was anything the legislature felt was good for the country; and just compensation came to be considered unnecessary if the government deliberately took and destroyed less than 100 percent of the individual's property.

Epstein explains how a legal system is weakened when courts use language to mean whatever they think it should mean. What good is a constitution if it can be reinterpreted to suit different individuals at different times? If government acts capriciously, and with an almost wanton disregard for the law (by reinterpreting that law whenever convenient), it sends a strong and destructive message to individuals about the law: A law that can change to suit different individuals at different times is a law not binding on anyone. Hence, it is not a law to be respected, but one to be used to the advantage of those clever enough to manipulate it. The solution, as advocated by Epstein, is clear. The law must be absolute. It must be interpreted in a way that promotes respect for the language. Obvious misinterpretations of the law, such as government's failure to pay just compensation when it takes an individual's property, should be corrected.

Frivolous Lawsuits and Punitive Damages

Frivolous lawsuits and unlimited punitive damages have become commonplace in the U.S. Lawyers have little incentive to carefully weigh the merits of lawsuits they enter into; it costs no more to file a frivolous lawsuit than to file a legitimate claim, and the potential *upside* of a frivolous suit is often great. Lawyers have every incentive to demand outrageous sums of money for their clients. In a personal injury case, the practice of demanding punitive damages as a multiple of medical bills creates an incentive to boost those bills as high as possible. In many cases, even if the plaintiff isn't expected to win, the threat of the time and expense of legal fees will create an incentive for the other party to settle the case. The greatest abuse in this area comes from the most powerful of plaintiffs: government. The IRS or any other branch of government has the power to intimidate almost any defendant into settling rather than undergo the time and expense of a lengthy court case.

To address the problem of frivolous lawsuits and skyrocketing punitive damage awards, our legal system should incorporate some aspect of the "loser pays" rule from English law, which requires the losing party in a lawsuit to pay the court costs of the winner. In addition, we need objective criteria for establishing the amount of damage awards, and also for determining who should be made to pay those awards. Our current system—which determines awards based on a jury's sympathy for the victim, and assesses blame based on ability to pay rather than fault—

represents a travesty of justice and a violation of individual rights.

Cruel and Unusual Punishment

The constitutional prohibition against cruel and unusual punishment also has been abused. A judge in Georgia ruled that a prison's lack of cable TV and air conditioning constituted a violation of this constitutional protection. That case and countless others have severely undermined the present legal system. In the process, waste, fraud, and disrespect for the legal system have increased.

Each time a judge exercises personal judgment in lieu of strict legal interpretation, sides with the criminal at the expense of the victim, or allows cases to exceed the limits of common sense, he or she does a great injustice to the system.

The Benefits of Legal Reform

A recent study by Tillinghast, "Tort Cost Trends: An International Perspective," found that the cost of the U.S. tort system reached $152 billion in 1994. This amounts to 2.2 percent of gross domestic product. The study noted that the U.S. tort system is the most expensive in the industrialized world, at two-and-one-half times the average. Most industrialized countries have tort systems that cost less than 1 percent of their gross domestic product. Easily half of the costs associated with the U.S. tort system are pure waste. Those costs can be attributed to frivolous lawsuits and personal, subjective interpretations of the law. Adjusting the tort system so that the loser pays for court costs (or at least some portion of those costs) could save $75 billion, the equivalent of $625 per worker each year.

Adding the savings from tort reform to those we achieved in earlier chapters would bring the lowest-paid 17-year-old worker's yearly wage to just over $13,700. With this increase, the total retirement assets of the lowest-paid worker at age 67 would rise by roughly $27,000. This brings the total value of the lowest-paid worker's retirement assets to nearly $1,070,000.

Economic Impact on Lowest-Paid Worker: Legal Reform			
Annual Income at Age 17	+$625	Annual Income at Age 67	+$1,700
Retirement Account at Age 17	+$64	Retirement Account at Age 67	+$27,000

Annual Income of Lowest-Paid Worker:
Wage Plus Savings from Reforms

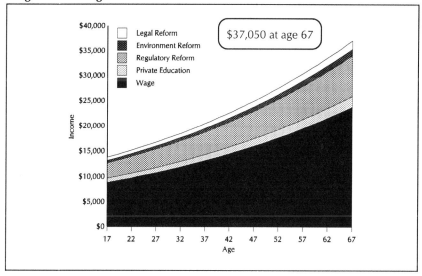

Legend:
- Legal Reform
- Environment Reform
- Regulatory Reform
- Private Education
- Wage

$37,050 at age 67

Retirement Assets of Lowest-Paid Worker:
Legal Reform

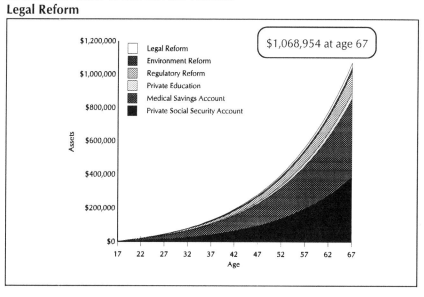

Legend:
- Legal Reform
- Environment Reform
- Regulatory Reform
- Private Education
- Medical Savings Account
- Private Social Security Account

$1,068,954 at age 67

PART FOUR

*Our Legacy to
the Next Generation*

Chapter 9

A NATION OF
MILLIONAIRES!

If all of the reforms noted in the previous chapters were carried out, the lowest-paid worker in the United States would retire with more than one million dollars in investable assets!

The first and most powerful reform is privatization of Social Security. This one reform would enable more than half of the nation's workers to retire with a million dollars in investable assets. As powerful as this reform would be, however, it would leave the lowest-paid worker with only a little over $380,000. That's $380,000 more than that person would have under the present Social Security arrangement—but it's still far short of the objective of creating a nation of millionaires.

The second reform addresses the problems of our health care system. Reforms that empower individual patients would enable each relatively healthy worker to save an additional $1,500 a year in a personal medical savings account. These savings, along with the retirement account assets,

A NATION OF MILLIONAIRES

would boost the lowest-paid worker's assets to just over $855,000 by the time he or she retires at age 67.

Studies show that privatizing the education system would lower costs and improve student achievement, increasing the average worker's income by $800 a year. That wage increase allows even more money to be set aside in the worker's private retirement account, adding $35,000 to the account by age 67.

The country's inefficient, bureaucratic regulatory system costs each worker roughly $5,000 *after* allowing for the benefits achieved by those regulations. Regulatory reform would boost the lowest-paid worker's income by at least $3,000 per worker every year, adding a whopping $129,000 to his or her retirement account.

Environmental and legal reforms would add another $1,125 to each worker's annual income, and $48,000 to the worker's retirement account by age 67.

All told, reforms such as those proposed in earlier chapters would boost the annual income of the country's lowest-paid workers by approximately $5,000, enough to enable them to retire with over a million dollars in investable assets. Moreover, the figures used in each instance are fairly conservative. The actual savings would almost certainly be far greater than projected here.

The Bonus: Indirect Benefits

The objective of creating a nation of millionaires is not only achievable; it is obtainable many times over and much sooner than the above figures suggest. The reason is that the preceding estimates of the benefits of reform accounted for only the *direct* benefits, ignoring substantial indirect benefits that reform would achieve.

Studies estimating the impact of free-market solutions traditionally underestimate their real beneficial effects. Economist William Laffer reviewed estimates of expected gains from deregulation and compared them to estimates of actual gains. He found that studies conducted after deregulation consistently showed gains one-and-a-half to five times as large as pre-deregulation projections. Clearly, some things are missing from most studies of the cost of regulation.

One thing that is missing is the effect that different regulations have on each other. Regulations can work at cross-purposes to raise costs far beyond their direct impact. Laffer notes, for example, that government-mandated auto safety and pollution control devices not only add directly to the cost of a car, but also make it more difficult and more expensive for auto manufacturers to meet the government's fuel economy standards.

In addition, inefficiencies, whenever they exist, show that output and incomes could have been higher. If output and incomes had been higher, more savings and investment would have occurred. Productivity is higher and technological innovation faster in the absence of regulation. As time passes, the difference between what could have occurred and what actually occurred becomes greater and greater. In the extreme, the difference between living standards in the United States, and those in poverty-stricken Third-World countries, represents the ultimate measure of the direct and indirect consequences of the efficiencies enjoyed by the United States throughout its history. In the same way, the difference between current incomes, and what incomes would be like if many of the remaining inefficiencies were eliminated, would be enormous.

Peter Huber, who has analyzed the impact of legal costs, estimates that the indirect costs are double the direct costs. Laffer essentially agrees, estimating that indirect costs are one-and-a-half to two times the direct costs. However, since the impact of the indirect costs builds over time, it is impossible to provide a reasonable estimate without referring to the time period under consideration.

Since our time period is particularly long (we are concerned with the income earned over a lifetime), the impact of these indirect costs is likely to be many times the direct costs. And thus, the indirect positive effects of the reforms mentioned in previous chapters will make a nation of millionaires not only achievable, but achievable far sooner than any previous estimates would suggest.

Just to get a rough idea of how the interaction of greater efficiency and higher productivity would affect income and wealth, let's observe what happens when productivity trends deteriorate as they did in the period from 1965 to 1981. For the fifteen years prior to 1965, the nation's efficiency had increased at roughly 2.5 percent a year. For the next sixteen years, it increased at a rate of just over 1 percent a year, significantly impacting incomes and living standards.

By 1981, the effects of this slow-down amounted to a yearly loss of income in the United States of $400 billion in 1995 dollars. This lowered the compensation of the typical worker by more than $4,000 in 1981 alone. Even though productivity has improved somewhat in the years since 1981, the gap between what might have been and what actually is reached $1.3 trillion a year by 1995. In terms of worker incomes, the gap between what was and what could have been is roughly $10,000 a year for the typical worker.

This illustration shows how relatively small changes in efficiency, extended over long periods of time, can produce huge changes in incomes. If the reforms suggested in this book are put into place, it is likely that productivity will rebound sufficiently to recapture what might have been. This would mean a substantial boost in real wages. The lowest-paid worker's annual wages, in 1995 dollars, would go from $8,840 a year to over $25,000 by 2010. Assuming all the above-mentioned reforms were made and the dynamic effects kicked in as expected, the lowest-paid worker would be able to take early retirement and still be a millionaire. Those workers earning more than the minimum wage would have the option of retiring at much younger ages or becoming multi-millionaires.

Since the analysis presented here focuses on a single worker, it suggests two important things. First, if two lowest-paid workers formed a household, their income and wealth would double. Second, since the additional dollars would raise living standards substantially, if the household decided to have children, one of the parents could more easily afford to remain home with the children. Re-establishing stable families with adult role models at home would go a long way toward addressing the problems of "latch-key" children, gangs, and the increasingly violent, anti-social behavior exhibited by our young people.

Better Neighbors, Too

While each family would have to choose the degree of supervision it desires for its children, at least the family would have the income necessary for full-time parental supervision. To the extent that the cultural and social problems of the past two decades are tied to financial pressures and to a lack of parental supervision, creating a nation of millionaires will result in more than rich people. It will result in a nation of families that can choose to spend more time with each other, and a nation of families that will more closely supervise and nurture their children. Not only would the U.S. be a nation of millionaires, but they would be the type of millionaires we'd all like to have as friends and neighbors.

Chapter 10

GETTING IT DONE

The previous chapters highlight the power of the U.S. economy. It is so awesome that under the most conservative estimates, the policy changes discussed in this book would enable even the lowest-paid workers in the country to retire as millionaires. Only one question remains: How do we accomplish those reforms?

At first blush, the political attraction of this outcome appears unassailable. Politicians should rush to embrace it. The truth, however, is more sobering. Many individuals and groups are either beneficiaries of the current system or perceive themselves as beneficiaries. They will fight vigorously against any change in the status quo.

To implement the changes necessary to achieve a nation of millionaires, we must begin with an objective assessment of the likely reaction of those who feel threatened by our proposals. By objectively examining just what is at stake, we can separate valid objections to reform from fictitious, self-defensive claims. Next, our reform proposals should be designed to meet the self-interest of as many people as possible, and promoted to demonstrate where that interest really lies.

Privatizing Social Security

Two groups react violently against the idea of privatizing Social Security. The first group is made up of those who currently receive benefits or who are close to retirement. The second group is composed of those who will lose power as a result of privatization.

The first group, retirees, fear that any change in the program will reduce their benefits. That fear is not only unjustified, it is totally backwards. Without the privatization of Social Security, benefits *will* be eroded. This already has begun. Social Security benefits once were tax-free, under the assumption that taxes were already paid on the funds when the money was earned. Then, half of all benefits were taxed, under the assumption that half of the money was paid by employers. And now 85 percent of the benefits are taxed, under no meaningful assumption.

Any move to privatize Social Security must begin by reassuring those who are retired or nearing retirement that their hard-earned benefits will be paid in full. Once the government has committed itself to a certain payment, it is just and proper that it meet that obligation. The appropriate strategy with regard to this group is to make it aware that its interests are best served not by continuing the present system, but by altering it in such a way that its members receive the benefits they have been promised.

The second group of opponents to privatizing Social Security fear (quite correctly) that they will lose power and influence. It is in the narrow self-interest of these groups to keep the present system in place. We should recognize that the opposition to privatization from these groups has more to do with protecting their own interests than with serving the interests of workers.

Among the groups that will lose power are the political establishment, certain groups that purport to represent the interests of retirees, and certain labor unions.

The political establishment completely controls the present government-run Social Security system. It determines who gets paid, when, how much, and under what circumstances. A lot of power accompanies the authority to make those decisions. There is also a great deal of power associated with the ability of politicians to help their constituents cut through the red tape that entangles all such government programs. Shifting this power to individuals, by allowing them to own and control their retirement funds, would significantly reduce the power of the political establishment.

Groups that purport to represent the interests of the elderly similarly find that their power increases when the elderly confront the Social Security bureaucracy. The greater the problems they face, the more often the elderly turn to powerful lobbying groups to protect their interests. However, if the elderly all become millionaires, with their own retirement accounts and few bureaucratic hurdles, they will have less need for powerful lobbying groups to protect their interests.

Certain labor unions will also have less power when retirement accounts are controlled by individual workers. Unions that currently manage their members' pension accounts are likely to find that Social Security privatization leads to pressures to add those pension funds to each worker's personal retirement account. Doing so would give workers even more flexibility and control over their assets. The additional power that accrues to workers would come at the expense of the union bureaucrats who now control the pension funds. Moreover, unions whose membership presently includes those who work for the Social Security Administration will have fewer members thirty years from now if the system is gradually phased out.

An effective strategy for overcoming the potential loss of power to all these groups is to confront them openly on the issue. Politicians will lose a significant amount of power under a private retirement system. It will no longer be possible for them to reward their constituents by "solving" the bureaucratic problems that a government agency has created. The whole role of government eventually will be substantially less when retirement funds no longer flow through government. Certain special interest groups and unions will also lose power. However, all of the power that is lost by these groups reverts to individual workers.

Politicians ultimately owe whatever power they have to the individuals who vote for them. It is up to those individuals to convince their representatives to give up some amount of power—or lose it all by being voted out of office.

Health Care

Our strategy for reforming health care should be similar to that used to privatize Social Security. Unfortunately, in the case of health care reform, more groups are likely to view themselves as being adversely affected by meaningful reform. Placing more power in the hands of individuals through medical savings accounts will affect health insurance companies, health maintenance organizations, pharmaceutical companies, hospitals, physicians, benefit consultants, government administrators, and many others who would have to adjust to the discipline of market pressures.

On the other hand, the health care field already has gone through some wrenching adjustments in recent years in attempts to reduce or contain the cost of company insurance plans. Shifting to a system where the individual is the customer (rather than some bureaucrat) may proceed more smoothly than anyone might imagine.

Since the potential rewards from introducing market pressures to the health care system are substantial, the main strategy is to focus attention on those rewards. Over and above the monetary gains is the potential of reform to take life-and-death issues out of the hands of a faceless bureaucracy and put them back in the hands of the individuals involved. To effectively promote market-oriented reform of the health care system, we should focus on the increased control that individuals would gain to make decisions regarding their families' health.

Finally, a clear understanding of how a fairly minor change in the overall tax structure would solve the bulk of the system's problems could go a long way toward convincing people that this change is essential.

Educational Choice

The main barriers to the establishment of a voucher system for education are the powerful teacher unions. Here is the clearest example possible of the interests of a few overwhelming the interests of the great majority.

The most effective argument here must be the potential to save half of all education expenses while improving the quality of education, an irrefutable argument that eventually will win the day. The main strategy to move that day forward should be to publicize the research in this area. Every time a parent is frustrated by the lack of response from a public school, and every time a homeowner views a soaring property tax bill, they should be reminded that there is an alternative.

Research on the costs of public school education in Chicago and Milwaukee confirms that public schools often provide an inferior product at twice the cost. A free-market system would never tolerate such a situation. Only under the government-run public education system is this ridiculous outcome possible.

When confronted with this evidence, the education establishment responds by agreeing to reform itself. School districts attempt to contract out education to private providers or establish so-called magnet (showcase) schools. Parents and taxpayers should recognize these tactics for what they are: a diversion, a delaying tactic designed to extend the life of a dying system. To the extent the public is fooled by such tactics, taxpayers will continue to see their education tax dollars wasted. Unfortunately, that is only a fraction of the current system's true cost to society. The real cost is depriving our youth of the best education money can buy.

Regulatory Reform

Studies on the inefficiency and waste stemming from the current regulatory system point to the potential for significant gains. Those gains are achievable by a more systematic assessment of risks and a market-oriented approach to solutions. Few realize that the present system costs each worker $5,000 to $10,000 a year *over and above* the benefits they receive from regulation.

Simple common sense tells us that government should evaluate the cost of its programs and compare that cost to the expected benefits. No business could afford to do anything less. But government plays by a different set of rules than does the private sector. Rather than focus on costs and benefits, government responds to political pressure. The groups that provide the greatest pressure tend to receive what they want.

Giving a screaming child whatever he wants just to keep him quiet is no way to raise a family. It's also no way to run a government. Our current regulatory system costs so much and delivers so little precisely because government tends to respond to political pressures, rather than economic realities. That is also why we can expect real reform to be very difficult. The regulatory system has created multitudes of screaming children who will oppose fundamental change.

For that reason, effective reform of the regulatory system will not come from a piecemeal response to each regulatory problem. What is needed is fundamental change in the structure of the regulatory system itself. Each and every government program must be evaluated in terms of its costs and benefits. As the excessive costs of various programs become more readily apparent, the pressure for regulatory reform will build, and it will become increasingly difficult for the special interests to protect their own piece of the pie. Given the enormous benefits that would result for our economy and all its workers, regulatory reform will prove well worth the fight.

Tort Reform

It is becoming increasingly apparent, even to the casual observer, that our legal system faces serious problems. Reform is essential—not just to save money, but also to increase respect for the law and restore the notion of personal responsibility.

The main losers under a package of effective legal reforms would be lawyers. If laws are vague and subject to multiple interpretations, lawyers can have a field day with almost any case. The more precise the meaning of laws and the more consistent their interpretation, the less work there is for lawyers.

Unfortunately, lawyers are not only a powerful lobbying group, but most politicians and judges are lawyers. They have a natural affinity for their profession. They may also expect to return to that profession once they leave office.

For those reasons, meaningful legal reform may be the most difficult of all reforms to achieve. Our main ally in this battle will be the research organizations, who must continue to document the waste of the present system and show how this waste hurts the economy, individual workers, and their families. It must be demonstrated time and again that the special interest groups claiming to represent "the little guy" too often have only their own selfish interests at heart.

Knowledge: The Key to Reform

At each stage of the reform process, research is needed to assess the potential benefits of reform. The research referenced in this book suggests that the benefits of reform are far greater than most of us would have imagined. And yet, that research has barely scratched the surface.

In the years ahead, policy analysts should expand their measures of inefficiency and apply them to many more aspects of government involvement in the economy. They should carefully review the benefits achieved by previous reforms. The researchers and techniques that most accurately predicted the gains from past reforms should be used to assess the potential of new reform proposals.

Knowledge is the key to reform. The more we learn, the easier it will be for us to change those things that create inefficiencies and waste. It is one thing for a powerful special interest group to claim that current programs are in the public interest, and "just happen" to benefit the group's members at the same time. It is quite another thing for that special interest group to be confronted with careful research that shows how the programs are frittering away national resources and making workers and their families worse off than they should be.

The more studies that are done, and the more people are informed, the greater the pressure will be for meaningful reform. With meaningful reform in the policy areas discussed here, the next generation will grow up wiser, safer, and more prosperous than anyone might have imagined.

Chapter 11

SUMMING UP

This book began with a seemingly fantastic objective: to turn every worker in America into a millionaire. The first two chapters showed how existing government policies have been moving in the opposite direction. Instead of getting richer, most workers have become poorer. And not only have they become poorer, but the link between their actions and the responsibility for those actions has been weakened. This has meant the loss of a large part of the independence and responsibility that have characterized the American heritage.

As these trends have evolved, social and cultural indicators have revealed a steady deterioration. One can only wonder how many senseless, violent crimes are the indirect result of government policies that have weakened the link between an individual's actions and his responsibility for those actions. As a costly and growing government bureaucracy has placed increased financial pressure on individuals and families, personal conduct has been changed, and even the structure and intimacy of many families have been disrupted.

Government regulations and bureaucracy have diminished the respect individuals have for the law. They destroy the confidence individuals have in their own abilities. There can be few greater tasks facing the nation in the years ahead than reversing these trends.

The United States is the premier democracy in the world. Citizens have the ability to achieve the type of institutional structure they want. However, it takes time and effort to understand what politicians are doing. Most people would prefer to spend their time doing other things. Unfortunately, when citizens ignore the political process, they create a vacuum. Given the government's power to influence incomes, political vacuums do not last for long. Once they exist, they are quickly filled. Given the opportunity, there are countless individuals who are willing to use government programs to enrich themselves at the expense of others.

What needs to be done is clear. For those who wish to protect themselves and their children from the destructive potential of government, the most efficient course of action is to work to change the institutional structure. Each change that shifts power from government to individuals tends to diffuse the government's base of power. The more diffused power becomes, the more difficult it is for groups to harness that power for their own self-interests.

In recent years, many of the institutional changes mentioned in this book have begun to be openly debated. Unfortunately, many of the changes that have been proposed in the public debate would move the institutional structure only modestly in the directions suggested. For example, some have suggested that the Social Security system be changed so that a small percentage of each worker's salary goes into a private retirement account. While some is better than none, it is important to remember that moderate changes will bring about only moderate improvements. For those at the lower end of the income scale, modest changes are not enough. The bolder the changes, the sooner society can expect meaningful results.

While all of the institutional changes referred to in this book are important, the most important is the privatization of Social Security. While other reforms can substantially improve living standards, they cannot instill the sense of value, pride, independence, and responsibility that is associated with true financial independence as one approaches retirement. Only by privatizing Social Security will all workers be able to experience that independence.

This book provides the blueprint for a new society, a nation of millionaires. That nation would have individuals with greater financial independence and fewer financial pressures. There would be less strife, less crime, less pollution, and maybe even fewer lawyers. It is the type of society that promotes responsibility and provides substantial rewards to all workers.

That is a society worth working for.
It is a legacy we can be proud to leave for the next generation.

PART FIVE

Appendices

DATA

The numbers in the following tables show how even the much-maligned hamburger-flipper can become a millionaire. In fact, most hamburger-flippers make more than the lowest-paid worker, and would therefore be multi-millionaires.

The wage of the lowest-paid worker is set at the minimum wage of $4.25 an hour, purely for purposes of illustration. All wages, including the minimum wage, are ultimately determined by market forces, not by politicians. Just as passing legislation that seeks to make winter warmer and summer cooler will not change weather patterns, so legislation to raise or lower the minimum wage has little effect on wage patterns. When politicians legislate a minimum wage, they simply alter the supply of workers. If the legal minimum wage is close to the market minimum, then relatively few workers will be priced out of the market. The further the legal minimum wage is from the market minimum, the greater the number of potential workers who will be priced out of jobs.

I have assumed here that the 1996 legal minimum wage of $4.25 is close to the market minimum. Hence, setting the minimum wage at $5.00 or $6.00 an hour would not have the effect of producing more millionaires. Instead, it will simply prevent potential millionaires from getting started. The end result will be fewer, not more, millionaires.

I have also assumed that the minimum wage, as well as the income benefits from the reforms proposed here, will increase at a real rate of 2 percent per year. This increase reflects my view that productivity will rise at a rate of 2 percent a year. This is twice the rate at which productivity has increased during the past 25 years. However, productivity and living standards have performed so poorly largely because of the foolish moves to increase government interference in the economy. The institutional changes that are proposed in this book would enable productivity to grow at least 2 percent a year.

The assumption that the average retirement or medical savings account will earn a real return of 6 percent is also reasonable. Six percent is one percentage point less than the real return to stocks over long periods of time. Given the changes that would be occurring in the economy as a result of the reforms proposed here, stock prices are likely to rise faster than the historical average.

All things considered, the assumptions that allow for the creation of a nation of millionaires are fairly conservative. If the policy recommendations discussed in this book are implemented, there would be millionaires on every street corner much sooner than the following numbers suggest.

I'd bet a million on it.

Privatized Social Security
Assuming No Wage Increase

Age	Minimum Wage	Annual Contribution to Retirement Account	Contribution w/Interest	Net Benefit
17	$8,840	$884	$908	$908
18	$8,840	$884	$908	$1,871
19	$8,840	$884	$908	$2,891
20	$8,840	$884	$908	$3,973
21	$8,840	$884	$908	$5,119
22	$8,840	$884	$908	$6,334
23	$8,840	$884	$908	$7,623
24	$8,840	$884	$908	$8,988
25	$8,840	$884	$908	$10,435
26	$8,840	$884	$908	$11,970
27	$8,840	$884	$908	$13,596
28	$8,840	$884	$908	$15,320
29	$8,840	$884	$908	$17,147
30	$8,840	$884	$908	$19,084
31	$8,840	$884	$908	$21,137
32	$8,840	$884	$908	$23,313
33	$8,840	$884	$908	$25,620
34	$8,840	$884	$908	$28,066
35	$8,840	$884	$908	$30,658
36	$8,840	$884	$908	$33,405
37	$8,840	$884	$908	$36,318
38	$8,840	$884	$908	$39,405
39	$8,840	$884	$908	$42,677
40	$8,840	$884	$908	$46,146
41	$8,840	$884	$908	$49,823
42	$8,840	$884	$908	$53,721
43	$8,840	$884	$908	$57,852

Privatized Social Security
Assuming No Wage Increase

Age	Minimum Wage	Annual Contribution to Retirement Account	Contribution w/Interest	Net Benefit
44	$8,840	$884	$908	$62,231
45	$8,840	$884	$908	$66,873
46	$8,840	$884	$908	$71,794
47	$8,840	$884	$908	$77,009
48	$8,840	$884	$908	$82,538
49	$8,840	$884	$908	$88,398
50	$8,840	$884	$908	$94,610
51	$8,840	$884	$908	$101,195
52	$8,840	$884	$908	$108,175
53	$8,840	$884	$908	$115,573
54	$8,840	$884	$908	$123,416
55	$8,840	$884	$908	$131,729
56	$8,840	$884	$908	$140,541
57	$8,840	$884	$908	$149,881
58	$8,840	$884	$908	$159,782
59	$8,840	$884	$908	$170,278
60	$8,840	$884	$908	$181,402
61	$8,840	$884	$908	$193,195
62	$8,840	$884	$908	$205,694
63	$8,840	$884	$908	$218,944
64	$8,840	$884	$908	$232,989
65	$8,840	$884	$908	$247,876
66	$8,840	$884	$908	$263,657
67	$8,840	$884	$908	$280,384

Privatized Social Security
Assuming 2 Percent Annual Wage Increase

Age	Minimum Wage	Annual Contribution to Retirement Account	Contribution w/Interest	Net Benefit
17	$8,840	$884	$908	$908
18	$9,017	$902	$926	$1,889
19	$9,197	$920	$945	$2,947
20	$9,381	$938	$964	$4,088
21	$9,569	$957	$983	$5,316
22	$9,760	$976	$1,003	$6,637
23	$9,955	$996	$1,023	$8,058
24	$10,154	$1,015	$1,043	$9,585
25	$10,357	$1,036	$1,064	$11,224
26	$10,565	$1,056	$1,085	$12,983
27	$10,776	$1,078	$1,107	$14,869
28	$10,991	$1,099	$1,129	$16,890
29	$11,211	$1,121	$1,152	$19,055
30	$11,435	$1,144	$1,175	$21,373
31	$11,664	$1,166	$1,198	$23,854
32	$11,897	$1,190	$1,222	$26,507
33	$12,135	$1,214	$1,247	$29,344
34	$12,378	$1,238	$1,272	$32,376
35	$12,626	$1,263	$1,297	$35,616
36	$12,878	$1,288	$1,323	$39,076
37	$13,136	$1,314	$1,349	$42,770
38	$13,398	$1,340	$1,376	$46,712
39	$13,666	$1,367	$1,404	$50,919
40	$13,940	$1,394	$1,432	$55,406
41	$14,219	$1,422	$1,461	$60,191
42	$14,503	$1,450	$1,490	$65,292
43	$14,793	$1,479	$1,520	$70,730

Privatized Social Security
Assuming 2 Percent Annual Wage Increase

Age	Minimum Wage	Annual Contribution to Retirement Account	Contribution w/Interest	Net Benefit
44	$15,089	$1,509	$1,550	$76,523
45	$15,391	$1,539	$1,581	$82,696
46	$15,698	$1,570	$1,613	$89,270
47	$16,012	$1,601	$1,645	$96,271
48	$16,333	$1,633	$1,678	$103,725
49	$16,659	$1,666	$1,711	$111,660
50	$16,993	$1,699	$1,746	$120,105
51	$17,332	$1,733	$1,781	$129,092
52	$17,679	$1,768	$1,816	$138,654
53	$18,033	$1,803	$1,852	$148,826
54	$18,393	$1,839	$1,889	$159,645
55	$18,761	$1,876	$1,927	$171,151
56	$19,136	$1,914	$1,966	$183,386
57	$19,519	$1,952	$2,005	$196,394
58	$19,909	$1,991	$2,045	$210,223
59	$20,308	$2,031	$2,086	$224,922
60	$20,714	$2,071	$2,128	$240,545
61	$21,128	$2,113	$2,170	$257,149
62	$21,551	$2,155	$2,214	$274,791
63	$21,982	$2,198	$2,258	$293,537
64	$22,421	$2,242	$2,303	$313,452
65	$22,870	$2,287	$2,349	$334,609
66	$23,327	$2,333	$2,396	$357,082
67	$23,794	$2,379	$2,444	$380,951

Medical Savings Accounts

Age	Annual Contribution	Contribution w/Interest	Net Benefit
17	$1,500	$1,541	$1,541
18	$1,500	$1,541	$3,174
19	$1,500	$1,541	$4,906
20	$1,500	$1,541	$6,741
21	$1,500	$1,541	$8,686
22	$1,500	$1,541	$10,748
23	$1,500	$1,541	$12,934
24	$1,500	$1,541	$15,251
25	$1,500	$1,541	$17,707
26	$1,500	$1,541	$20,310
27	$1,500	$1,541	$23,070
28	$1,500	$1,541	$25,995
29	$1,500	$1,541	$29,096
30	$1,500	$1,541	$32,382
31	$1,500	$1,541	$35,866
32	$1,500	$1,541	$39,559
33	$1,500	$1,541	$43,474
34	$1,500	$1,541	$47,623
35	$1,500	$1,541	$52,021
36	$1,500	$1,541	$56,683
37	$1,500	$1,541	$61,625
38	$1,500	$1,541	$66,864
39	$1,500	$1,541	$72,416
40	$1,500	$1,541	$78,302
41	$1,500	$1,541	$84,541
42	$1,500	$1,541	$91,155
43	$1,500	$1,541	$98,165
44	$1,500	$1,541	$105,596
45	$1,500	$1,541	$113,472
46	$1,500	$1,541	$121,822
47	$1,500	$1,541	$130,672

Medical Savings Accounts

Age	Annual Contribution	Contribution w/Interest	Net Benefit
48	$1,500	$1,541	$140,053
49	$1,500	$1,541	$149,997
50	$1,500	$1,541	$160,538
51	$1,500	$1,541	$171,711
52	$1,500	$1,541	$183,555
53	$1,500	$1,541	$196,109
54	$1,500	$1,541	$209,416
55	$1,500	$1,541	$223,522
56	$1,500	$1,541	$238,474
57	$1,500	$1,541	$254,324
58	$1,500	$1,541	$271,124
59	$1,500	$1,541	$288,932
60	$1,500	$1,541	$307,809
61	$1,500	$1,541	$327,819
62	$1,500	$1,541	$349,029
63	$1,500	$1,541	$371,511
64	$1,500	$1,541	$395,343
65	$1,500	$1,541	$420,605
66	$1,500	$1,541	$447,382
67	$1,500	$1,541	$475,766

Private Education

Age	Additional Income	Annual Contribution	Contribution w/Interest	Net Benefit
17	$800	$80	$82	$82
18	$816	$82	$84	$171
19	$832	$83	$86	$267
20	$849	$85	$87	$370
21	$866	$87	$89	$481
22	$883	$88	$91	$601
23	$901	$90	$93	$729
24	$919	$92	$94	$867
25	$937	$94	$96	$1,016
26	$956	$96	$98	$1,175
27	$975	$98	$100	$1,346
28	$995	$99	$102	$1,528
29	$1,015	$101	$104	$1,724
30	$1,035	$103	$106	$1,934
31	$1,056	$106	$108	$2,159
32	$1,077	$108	$111	$2,399
33	$1,098	$110	$113	$2,656
34	$1,120	$112	$115	$2,930
35	$1,143	$114	$117	$3,223
36	$1,165	$117	$120	$3,536
37	$1,189	$119	$122	$3,871
38	$1,213	$121	$125	$4,227
39	$1,237	$124	$127	$4,608
40	$1,262	$126	$130	$5,014
41	$1,287	$129	$132	$5,447
42	$1,312	$131	$135	$5,909
43	$1,339	$134	$138	$6,401
44	$1,366	$137	$140	$6,925
45	$1,393	$139	$143	$7,484
46	$1,421	$142	$146	$8,079
47	$1,449	$145	$149	$8,712

Private Education

Age	Additional Income	Annual Contribution	Contribution w/Interest	Net Benefit
48	$1,478	$148	$152	$9,387
49	$1,508	$151	$155	$10,105
50	$1,538	$154	$158	$10,869
51	$1,569	$157	$161	$11,683
52	$1,600	$160	$164	$12,548
53	$1,632	$163	$168	$13,468
54	$1,665	$166	$171	$14,447
55	$1,698	$170	$174	$15,489
56	$1,732	$173	$178	$16,596
57	$1,766	$177	$181	$17,773
58	$1,802	$180	$185	$19,025
59	$1,838	$184	$189	$20,355
60	$1,875	$187	$193	$21,769
61	$1,912	$191	$196	$23,271
62	$1,950	$195	$200	$24,868
63	$1,989	$199	$204	$26,564
64	$2,029	$203	$208	$28,367
65	$2,070	$207	$213	$30,281
66	$2,111	$211	$217	$32,315
67	$2,153	$215	$221	$34,475

Regulatory Reform

Age	Additional Income	Annual Contribution	Contribution w/Interest	Net Benefit
17	$3,000	$300	$308	$308
18	$3,060	$306	$314	$641
19	$3,121	$312	$321	$1,000
20	$3,184	$318	$327	$1,387
21	$3,247	$325	$334	$1,804
22	$3,312	$331	$340	$2,252
23	$3,378	$338	$347	$2,735
24	$3,446	$345	$354	$3,253
25	$3,515	$351	$361	$3,809
26	$3,585	$359	$368	$4,406
27	$3,657	$366	$376	$5,046
28	$3,730	$373	$383	$5,732
29	$3,805	$380	$391	$6,467
30	$3,881	$388	$399	$7,253
31	$3,958	$396	$407	$8,095
32	$4,038	$404	$415	$8,996
33	$4,118	$412	$423	$9,958
34	$4,201	$420	$432	$10,987
35	$4,285	$428	$440	$12,087
36	$4,370	$437	$449	$13,261
37	$4,458	$446	$458	$14,515
38	$4,547	$455	$467	$15,853
39	$4,638	$464	$476	$17,280
40	$4,731	$473	$486	$18,803
41	$4,825	$483	$496	$20,427
42	$4,922	$492	$506	$22,158
43	$5,020	$502	$516	$24,003
44	$5,121	$512	$526	$25,969
45	$5,223	$522	$537	$28,064
46	$5,328	$533	$547	$30,295
47	$5,434	$543	$558	$32,671

Regulatory Reform

Age	Additional Income	Annual Contribution	Contribution w/Interest	Net Benefit
48	$5,543	$554	$569	$35,201
49	$5,654	$565	$581	$37,894
50	$5,767	$577	$592	$40,760
51	$5,882	$588	$604	$43,810
52	$6,000	$600	$616	$47,055
53	$6,120	$612	$629	$50,506
54	$6,242	$624	$641	$54,178
55	$6,367	$637	$654	$58,083
56	$6,494	$649	$667	$62,235
57	$6,624	$662	$680	$66,649
58	$6,757	$676	$694	$71,343
59	$6,892	$689	$708	$76,331
60	$7,030	$703	$722	$81,633
61	$7,170	$717	$737	$87,268
62	$7,314	$731	$751	$93,255
63	$7,460	$746	$766	$99,617
64	$7,609	$761	$782	$106,375
65	$7,761	$776	$797	$113,555
66	$7,916	$792	$813	$121,182
67	$8,075	$807	$829	$129,282

Environment Reform

Age	Additional Income	Annual Contribution	Contribution w/Interest	Net Benefit
17	$500	$50	$51	$51
18	$510	$51	$52	$107
19	$520	$52	$53	$167
20	$531	$53	$55	$231
21	$541	$54	$56	$301
22	$552	$55	$57	$375
23	$563	$56	$58	$456
24	$574	$57	$59	$542
25	$586	$59	$60	$635
26	$598	$60	$61	$734
27	$609	$61	$63	$841
28	$622	$62	$64	$955
29	$634	$63	$65	$1,078
30	$647	$65	$66	$1,209
31	$660	$66	$68	$1,349
32	$673	$67	$69	$1,499
33	$686	$69	$71	$1,660
34	$700	$70	$72	$1,831
35	$714	$71	$73	$2,014
36	$728	$73	$75	$2,210
37	$743	$74	$76	$2,419
38	$758	$76	$78	$2,642
39	$773	$77	$79	$2,880
40	$788	$79	$81	$3,134
41	$804	$80	$83	$3,404
42	$820	$82	$84	$3,693
43	$837	$84	$86	$4,001
44	$853	$85	$88	$4,328
45	$871	$87	$89	$4,677
46	$888	$89	$91	$5,049
47	$906	$91	$93	$5,445

Environment Reform

Age	Additional Income	Annual Contribution	Contribution w/Interest	Net Benefit
48	$924	$92	$95	$5,867
49	$942	$94	$97	$6,316
50	$961	$96	$99	$6,793
51	$980	$98	$101	$7,302
52	$1,000	$100	$103	$7,842
53	$1,020	$102	$105	$8,418
54	$1,040	$104	$107	$9,030
55	$1,061	$106	$109	$9,680
56	$1,082	$108	$111	$10,372
57	$1,104	$110	$113	$11,108
58	$1,126	$113	$116	$11,890
59	$1,149	$115	$118	$12,722
60	$1,172	$117	$120	$13,605
61	$1,195	$120	$123	$14,545
62	$1,219	$122	$125	$15,542
63	$1,243	$124	$128	$16,603
64	$1,268	$127	$130	$17,729
65	$1,294	$129	$133	$18,926
66	$1,319	$132	$136	$20,197
67	$1,346	$135	$138	$21,547

Legal Reform

Age	Additional Income	Annual Contribution	Contribution w/Interest	Net Benefit
17	$625	$63	$64	$64
18	$638	$64	$65	$134
19	$650	$65	$67	$208
20	$663	$66	$68	$289
21	$677	$68	$69	$376
22	$690	$69	$71	$469
23	$704	$70	$72	$570
24	$718	$72	$74	$678
25	$732	$73	$75	$794
26	$747	$75	$77	$918
27	$762	$76	$78	$1,051
28	$777	$78	$80	$1,194
29	$793	$79	$81	$1,347
30	$809	$81	$83	$1,511
31	$825	$82	$85	$1,686
32	$841	$84	$86	$1,874
33	$858	$86	$88	$2,075
34	$875	$88	$90	$2,289
35	$893	$89	$92	$2,518
36	$911	$91	$94	$2,763
37	$929	$93	$95	$3,024
38	$947	$95	$97	$3,303
39	$966	$97	$99	$3,600
40	$986	$99	$101	$3,917
41	$1,005	$101	$103	$4,256
42	$1,025	$103	$105	$4,616
43	$1,046	$105	$107	$5,001
44	$1,067	$107	$110	$5,410
45	$1,088	$109	$112	$5,847
46	$1,110	$111	$114	$6,312
47	$1,132	$113	$116	$6,807

Legal Reform

Age	Additional Income	Annual Contribution	Contribution w/Interest	Net Benefit
48	$1,155	$115	$119	$7,334
49	$1,178	$118	$121	$7,895
50	$1,201	$120	$123	$8,492
51	$1,225	$123	$126	$9,127
52	$1,250	$125	$128	$9,803
53	$1,275	$127	$131	$10,522
54	$1,300	$130	$134	$11,287
55	$1,326	$133	$136	$12,101
56	$1,353	$135	$139	$12,966
57	$1,380	$138	$142	$13,885
58	$1,408	$141	$145	$14,863
59	$1,436	$144	$147	$15,902
60	$1,464	$146	$150	$17,007
61	$1,494	$149	$153	$18,181
62	$1,524	$152	$157	$19,428
63	$1,554	$155	$160	$20,753
64	$1,585	$159	$163	$22,162
65	$1,617	$162	$166	$23,657
66	$1,649	$165	$169	$25,246
67	$1,682	$168	$173	$26,934

Summary: Impact of Reforms on Income of Lowest-Paid Worker

Age	Minimum Wage 2% Growth	Private Education	Regulatory Reform	Environment Reform	Legal Reform	Total Income
17	$8,840	$800	$3,000	$500	$625	$13,765
18	$9,017	$816	$3,060	$510	$638	$14,040
19	$9,197	$832	$3,121	$520	$650	$14,321
20	$9,381	$849	$3,184	$531	$663	$14,608
21	$9,569	$866	$3,247	$541	$677	$14,900
22	$9,760	$883	$3,312	$552	$690	$15,198
23	$9,955	$901	$3,378	$563	$704	$15,502
24	$10,154	$919	$3,446	$574	$718	$15,812
25	$10,357	$937	$3,515	$586	$732	$16,128
26	$10,565	$956	$3,585	$598	$747	$16,450
27	$10,776	$975	$3,657	$609	$762	$16,779
28	$10,991	$995	$3,730	$622	$777	$17,115
29	$11,211	$1,015	$3,805	$634	$793	$17,457
30	$11,435	$1,035	$3,881	$647	$809	$17,806
31	$11,664	$1,056	$3,958	$660	$825	$18,163
32	$11,897	$1,077	$4,038	$673	$841	$18,526
33	$12,135	$1,098	$4,118	$686	$858	$18,896
34	$12,378	$1,120	$4,201	$700	$875	$19,274

Summary: Impact of Reforms on Income of Lowest-Paid Worker

Age	Minimum Wage 2% Growth	Private Education	Regulatory Reform	Environment Reform	Legal Reform	Total Income
35	$12,626	$1,143	$4,285	$714	$893	$19,660
36	$12,878	$1,165	$4,370	$728	$911	$20,053
37	$13,136	$1,189	$4,458	$743	$929	$20,454
38	$13,398	$1,213	$4,547	$758	$947	$20,863
39	$13,666	$1,237	$4,638	$773	$966	$21,280
40	$13,940	$1,262	$4,731	$788	$986	$21,706
41	$14,219	$1,287	$4,825	$804	$1,005	$22,140
42	$14,503	$1,312	$4,922	$820	$1,025	$22,583
43	$14,793	$1,339	$5,020	$837	$1,046	$23,035
44	$15,089	$1,366	$5,121	$853	$1,067	$23,495
45	$15,391	$1,393	$5,223	$871	$1,088	$23,965
46	$15,698	$1,421	$5,328	$888	$1,110	$24,445
47	$16,012	$1,449	$5,434	$906	$1,132	$24,933
48	$16,333	$1,478	$5,543	$924	$1,155	$25,432
49	$16,659	$1,508	$5,654	$942	$1,178	$25,941
50	$16,993	$1,538	$5,767	$961	$1,201	$26,460
51	$17,332	$1,569	$5,882	$980	$1,225	$26,989
52	$17,679	$1,600	$6,000	$1,000	$1,250	$27,528

Summary: Impact of Reforms on
Income of Lowest-Paid Worker

Age	Minimum Wage 2% Growth	Private Education	Regulatory Reform	Environment Reform	Legal Reform	Total Income
53	$18,033	$1,632	$6,120	$1,020	$1,275	$28,079
54	$18,393	$1,665	$6,242	$1,040	$1,300	$28,641
55	$18,761	$1,698	$6,367	$1,061	$1,326	$29,213
56	$19,136	$1,732	$6,494	$1,082	$1,353	$29,798
57	$19,519	$1,766	$6,624	$1,104	$1,380	$30,394
58	$19,909	$1,802	$6,757	$1,126	$1,408	$31,002
59	$20,308	$1,838	$6,892	$1,149	$1,436	$31,622
60	$20,714	$1,875	$7,030	$1,172	$1,464	$32,254
61	$21,128	$1,912	$7,170	$1,195	$1,494	$32,899
62	$21,551	$1,950	$7,314	$1,219	$1,524	$33,557
63	$21,982	$1,989	$7,460	$1,243	$1,554	$34,228
64	$22,421	$2,029	$7,609	$1,268	$1,585	$34,913
65	$22,870	$2,070	$7,761	$1,294	$1,617	$35,611
66	$23,327	$2,111	$7,916	$1,319	$1,649	$36,323
67	$23,794	$2,153	$8,075	$1,346	$1,682	$37,050

Summary: Impact of Reforms on Retirement Assets

Age	10% from Wage	Private Education	Regulatory Reform	Environment Reform	Legal Reform	Total in Retirement Account	Total in Medical Savings Account	Total Investable Assets
17	$908	$82	$308	$51	$64	$1,413	$1,541	$2,954
18	$1,889	$171	$641	$107	$134	$2,942	$3,174	$6,116
19	$2,947	$267	$1,000	$167	$208	$4,589	$4,906	$9,495
20	$4,088	$370	$1,387	$231	$289	$6,365	$6,741	$13,106
21	$5,316	$481	$1,804	$301	$376	$8,278	$8,686	$16,964
22	$6,637	$601	$2,252	$375	$469	$10,334	$10,748	$21,082
23	$8,058	$729	$2,735	$456	$570	$12,548	$12,934	$25,482
24	$9,585	$867	$3,253	$542	$678	$14,925	$15,251	$30,176
25	$11,224	$1,016	$3,809	$635	$794	$17,478	$17,707	$35,185
26	$12,983	$1,175	$4,406	$734	$918	$20,216	$20,310	$40,526
27	$14,869	$1,346	$5,046	$841	$1,051	$23,153	$23,070	$46,223
28	$16,890	$1,528	$5,732	$955	$1,194	$26,299	$25,995	$52,294
29	$19,055	$1,724	$6,467	$1,078	$1,347	$29,671	$29,096	$58,767
30	$21,373	$1,934	$7,253	$1,209	$1,511	$33,280	$32,382	$65,662
31	$23,854	$2,159	$8,095	$1,209	$1,686	$37,143	$35,866	$73,009
32	$26,507	$2,399	$8,996	$1,499	$1,874	$41,275	$39,559	$80,834
33	$29,344	$2,656	$9,958	$1,660	$2,075	$45,693	$43,474	$89,167
34	$32,376	$2,930	$10,987	$1,831	$2,289	$50,413	$47,623	$98,036
35	$35,616	$3,223	$12,087	$2,014	$2,518	$55,458	$52,021	$107,479
36	$39,076	$3,536	$13,261	$2,210	$2,763	$60,846	$56,683	$117,529
37	$42,770	$3,871	$14,515	$2,419	$3,024	$66,599	$61,625	$128,224

Summary: Impact of Reforms on Retirement Assets

Age	10% from Wage	Private Education	Regulatory Reform	Environment Reform	Legal Reform	Total in Retirement Account	Total in Medical Savings Account	Total Investable Assets
38	$46,712	$4,227	$15,853	$2,642	$3,303	$72,737	$66,864	$139,601
39	$50,919	$4,608	$17,280	$2,880	$3,600	$79,287	$72,416	$151,703
40	$55,406	$5,014	$18,803	$3,134	$3,917	$86,274	$78,302	$164,576
41	$60,191	$5,447	$20,427	$3,404	$4,256	$93,725	$84,541	$178,266
42	$65,292	$5,909	$22,158	$3,693	$4,616	$101,668	$91,155	$192,823
43	$70,730	$6,401	$24,003	$4,001	$5,001	$110,136	$98,165	$208,301
44	$76,523	$6,925	$25,969	$4,328	$5,410	$119,155	$105,596	$224,751
45	$82,696	$7,484	$28,064	$4,677	$5,847	$128,768	$113,472	$242,240
46	$89,270	$8,079	$30,295	$5,049	$6,312	$139,005	$121,822	$260,827
47	$96,271	$8,712	$32,671	$5,445	$6,807	$149,906	$130,672	$280,578
48	$103,725	$9,387	$35,201	$5,867	$7,334	$161,514	$140,053	$301,567
49	$111,660	$10,105	$37,894	$6,316	$7,895	$173,870	$149,997	$323,867
50	$120,105	$10,869	$40,760	$6,793	$8,492	$187,019	$160,538	$347,557
51	$129,092	$11,683	$43,810	$7,302	$9,127	$201,014	$171,711	$372,725
52	$138,654	$12,548	$47,055	$7,842	$9,803	$215,902	$183,555	$399,457
53	$148,826	$13,468	$50,506	$8,418	$10,522	$231,740	$196,109	$427,849
54	$159,645	$14,447	$54,178	$9,030	$11,287	$248,587	$209,416	$458,003
55	$171,151	$15,489	$58,083	$9,680	$12,101	$266,504	$223,522	$490,026
56	$183,386	$16,596	$62,235	$10,372	$12,966	$285,555	$238,474	$524,029
57	$196,394	$17,773	$66,649	$11,108	$13,885	$305,809	$254,324	$560,133
58	$210,223	$19,025	$71,343	$11,890	$14,863	$327,344	$271,124	$598,468

Summary: Impact of Reforms on Retirement Assets

Age	10% from Wage	Private Education	Regulatory Reform	Environment Reform	Legal Reform	Total in Retirement Account	Total in Medical Savings Account	Total Investable Assets
59	$224,922	$20,355	$76,331	$12,722	$15,902	$350,232	$288,932	$639,164
60	$240,545	$21,769	$81,633	$13,605	$17,007	$374,559	$307,809	$682,368
61	$257,149	$23,271	$87,268	$14,545	$18,181	$400,414	$327,819	$728,233
62	$274,791	$24,868	$93,255	$15,542	$19,428	$427,884	$349,029	$776,913
63	$293,537	$26,564	$99,617	$16,603	$20,753	$457,074	$371,511	$828,585
64	$313,452	$28,367	$106,375	$17,729	$22,162	$488,085	$395,343	$883,428
65	$334,609	$30,281	$113,555	$18,926	$23,657	$521,028	$420,605	$941,633
66	$357,082	$32,315	$121,182	$20,197	$25,246	$556,022	$447,382	$1,003,404
67	$380,951	$34,475	$129,282	$21,547	$26,934	$593,189	$475,766	$1,068,955

BIBLIOGRAPHY

Anderson, Terry L. and Donald R. Leal. *Free Market Environmentalism*. San Francisco, California: Pacific Research Institute for Public Policy, 1991.

Baden, John A., editor. *Environmental Gore*. San Francisco, California: Pacific Research Institute for Public Policy, 1994.

Bailey, Ronald. *Eco-Scam*. New York, New York: St. Martin's Press, 1993.

_____ , editor. *The True State of the Planet*. New York, New York: The Free Press, 1995.

Barlett, Donald L. and James B. Steele. *America: What Went Wrong?* Kansas City, Missouri: Andrews and McMeel, 1992.

Bast, Joseph and Diane Bast, editors. *Rebuilding America's Schools*. Chicago, Illinois: The Heartland Institute, 1991.

Bast, Joseph, Peter J. Hill and Richard C. Rue. *Eco-Sanity*. Lanham, Maryland: Madison Books, 1994.

Bast, Joseph, Richard C. Rue and Stuart A. Wesbury. *Why We Spend Too Much on Health Care*. Chicago, Illinois: The Heartland Institute, 1993.

Bennett, William J. *The Index of Leading Cultural Indicators*. Washington, D.C.: The Heritage Foundation and Empower America, 1993.

Bernstam, Mikhail S. *The Wealth of Nations and the Environment*. London: Institute of Economic Affairs, 1991.

Bluestone, Barry and Bennett Harrison. *The Deindustrialization of America*. New York, New York: Basic Books, 1982.

Bovard, James. *The Fair Trade Fraud*. New York, New York: St. Martin's Press, 1991.

_____ . *The Farm Fiasco*. San Francisco, Caifornia: ICS Press, 1989.

Brown, Larry and H. F. Pizer. *Living Hungry in America*. New York, New York: New American Library, 1987.

Chilton, Kenneth and Melinda Warren. *Environmental Protection: Regulating for Results*. Boulder, Colorado: Westview Press, 1991.

Chubb, John E. and Terry M. Moe. *Politics, Markets & America's Schools*. Washington, D.C.: The Brookings Institution, 1990.

Cihak, Robert J. *Medical Savings Accounts: A Building Block for Sound Health Care*. Olympia, Washington: Evergreen Freedom Foundation, 1995.

Cox, Wendell. "Competition: The Prerequisite for Improved Public Transit." Presentation to the American Legislative Exchange Council, Colorado Springs, Colorado, August 6, 1992.

Easterbrook, Gregg. *A Moment on the Earth*. New York, New York: Viking Penguin, 1995.

Epstein, Richard A. *Takings: Private Property and the Power of Eminent Domain*. Cambridge, Massachusetts: Harvard University Press, 1985.

Feldstein, Martin. "The Missing Piece in Policy Analysis: Social Security Reform." The Richard T. Ely Lecture to the American Economic Association, Cambridge, Massachusetts, January 5, 1996.

Ferrara, Peter J., editor. *Social Security: Prospects for Real Reform*. Washington, D.C.: Cato Institute, 1985.

——————. *Social Security: Averting the Crisis*. Washington, D.C.: Cato Institute, 1982.

Friedman, Milton. *Capitalism & Freedom*. Chicago, Illinois: The University of Chicago Press, 1962.

Friedman, Milton and Rose Friedman. *Free to Choose*. New York, New York: Avon Books, 1981.

Fumento, Michael. *Science under Siege*. New York, New York: William Morrow and Company, Inc., 1993.

Genetski, Robert. *A Fiscal Analysis of Public and Private Education*. Chicago, Illinois: Chicago Capital, 1992.

_____ . "Private Schools, Public Savings." *The Wall Street Journal*, July 8, 1992.

_____ . "Privatize Social Security." *The Wall Street Journal*, May 21, 1993.

_____ . *Taking the Voodoo out of Economics*. Lake Bluff, Illinois: Regnery Books, 1986.

Gilder, George. *Wealth and Poverty*. New York, New York: Basic Books, 1981.

Goodman, John C. and Peter J. Ferrara. *Policy Alternatives to Social Security in Other Countries*. Dallas, Texas: National Center for Policy Analysis, 1988.

Goodman, John C. and Gerald L. Musgrave. *Patient Power*. Washington, D.C.: Cato Institute, 1994.

Gore, Albert. *Earth in the Balance*. New York, New York: Plume, 1993.

BIBLIOGRAPHY

Hall, Robert E. and Alvin Rabushka. *The Flat Tax.* Stanford, California: Hoover Institution Press, second edition, 1995.

Harmer, David. *School Choice: Why You Need It—How You Get It.* Washington, D.C.: Cato Institute, 1994.

Harrison, Bennett and Barry Bluestone. *The Great U-Turn.* New York, New York: Basic Books, 1988.

Hood, John. "OSHA's Trivial Pursuit." *Policy Review,* Summer 1995.

Hopkins, Thomas D. "The Costs of Federal Regulation." *Journal of Regulation and Social Costs,* Volume 2, Number 1, March 1992.

_____ . "Costs of Regulation: Filling the Gaps." Report for Regulatory Information Service Center, August 1992.

_____ . "Federal Regulatory Burdens: An Overview." Rochester Institute of Technology Public Policy Working Paper, 1993.

Huber, Peter. *Liability: The Legal Revolution and Its Consequences.* New York, New York: Basic Books, 1988.

Laffer, William G. "The Costs of Regulation." (unpublished paper)

Lave, Lester B. *How Safe Is Safe Enough?* St. Louis, Missouri: Center for the Study of American Business, 1990.

Lehr, Jay H., editor. *Rational Readings on Environmental Concerns.* New York, New York: Van Nostrand Reinhold, 1992.

Meiners, Roger E. and Bruce Yandle, editors. *Regulation and the Reagan Era*. New York, New York: Homes & Meier Publishers, 1989.

Murray, Charles. *Losing Ground: American Social Policy 1950-1980*. New York, New York: Basic Books, 1984.

Novak, Michael. *The Spirit of Democratic Capitalism*. New York, New York: Simon and Schuster, 1982.

Phillips, Kevin. *The Politics of Rich and Poor*. New York, New York: Harper Perennial, 1991.

Public Policy Forum. *Public and Private School Costs: A Local Analysis*. Milwaukee, Wisconsin, 1994.

Ray, Dixy Lee. *Environmental Overkill*. Washington, D.C.: Regnery Gateway, 1993.

Reich, Robert B. *The Resurgent Liberal*. New York, New York: Vintage Books, 1991.

Seuss, Dr. *If I Ran the Circus*. New York, New York: Random House, 1956.

Shanahan, John C. and Adam D. Thierer. *How to Talk about Risk: How Well-Intentioned Regulations Can Kill*. Washington, D.C.: The Heritage Foundation, 1996.

Sheaffer, John R. and Leonard A. Stevens. *Future Water*. New York, New York: William Morrow & Co., 1983.

Thurow, Lester C. *Dangerous Currents: The State of Economics.*
New York, New York: Random House, 1983.

_____ . *The Zero-Sum Solution.* New York, New York: Simon
and Schuster, 1985.

Tillinghast. *Tort Cost Trends: An International Perspective.* Hartford,
Connecticut: Tower Perrin, 1995.

Weidenbaum, Murray and Melinda Warren. *It's Time to Cut Government Regulations.* St. Louis, Missouri: Center for the Study of
American Business, 1995.

World Bank. *The East Asian Miracle: Economic Growth and Public
Policy.* New York, New York: Oxford University Press, 1993.

INDEX

incentives 17
  and environment
    doomsayers 84-85
income 19-20
  earnings over time 19
  impact of reform on 43,
    68-70, 74-77, 92-95,
    101-3, 129-32, 135-45
  impact of regulation on 74
  minimum wage 127-28
inefficiency
  impact on economy 110

labor unions 115, 116, 117
Laffer, William 74, 75, 108,
    109
legal system
  abuse of 98-101
  cost of 98, 101
  costs versus benefits 98
  cruel and unusual
    punishment 101
  and culture 98
  and frivolous lawsuits 100
  necessity of 98
  and punitive damages 100
  and subjectivity 99-101
  and values 98
legal system reform 97
  impact on income 101-3,
    108, 141-42
  impact on retirement
    accounts 102, 103,
    108, 141-42
  loser pays 100
  obstacles to 119

Living Hungry in America
    (Brown and Pizer) 12
Losing Ground (Murray) 11

managed care 47
Medicaid 47, 48
  failure of 48
  reform of 53
medical savings accounts 50-
    52
  and catastrophic insurance
    51
  and cost containment 54,
    55, 59
  and cost-consciousness 54
  and the elderly 53
  and the poor 53
  value of 55-58, 133-34
Medicare 47, 48
  failure of 48
  reform of 53
moral values 10-11, 17, 18,
    121
Murray, Charles 11
Musgrave, Gerald 46, 47, 55

National Center for Policy
    Analysis 9, 17

Occupational Safety and
    Health Administration
    72

parental choice
  and competition 68
  and cost containment 68

ABOUT THE AUTHOR

Robert J. Genetski, Ph.D., is one of the nation's premier interest rate forecasters and investment advisors. Formerly chief economist for Chicago's Harris Bank, he is now Senior Managing Director for Chicago Capital, Inc., an investment bank in Chicago. His responsibilities include directing the bank's investment research and asset management activities.

Dr. Genetski is a popular speaker who entertains thousands of people at conferences and investor meetings around the world each year. He is the recipient of the Illinois Public Policy Caucuses' *Timeless Truths* award, in recognition for his contributions to free-market economic research. In the late 1970s, he produced pioneering studies that showed how economic performance was influenced by changes in state and local taxes. His research was the first to discover what subsequent studies have confirmed: States that increase their taxes relative to other states tend to experience below-average economic performance, while states that reduce their relative taxes tend to experience above-average economic performance.

In the early 1980s, Dr. Genetski's research into the impact of tax changes on productivity correctly predicted rising productivity, rising living standards, and lower inflation as a consequence of the Reagan tax cuts. In the early 1990s, his research showed that Chicago-area private schools educated children for between 25 and 50 percent of the cost of public schools. A recent study of Milwaukee-area schools confirmed his findings.

Dr. Genetski has written several books and numerous articles. He is the author of *Taking the Voodoo out of Economics*, an influential book that anticipated and shaped many of the public policies hotly debated in Washington today. As a member of Blue Chip forecasters, Dr. Genetski has been commended on his ability to out-forecast the pack. In 1989 and again in 1994, he was ranked the number one interest rate forecaster, according to *Institutional Investor Magazine* and *Blue Chip Financial Forecasts*.

Dr. Genetski earned his Ph.D. in economics from New York University. He has taught economics at New York University and at the University of Chicago's Graduate School of Business. He is a policy advisor to The Heartland Institute, an Illinois-based public policy research organization. He serves on several boards of directors and writes a regular column for the *Nikkei Financial Daily*, Japan's leading business newspaper.

ABOUT
THE HEARTLAND INSTITUTE

The Heartland Institute is a nonprofit public policy research organization serving the nation's eight thousand federal and state elected officials, journalists, Heartland Members, and other opinion leaders.

Founded in 1984, Heartland was the first think tank in the nation to focus on free-market solutions to state and local public policy problems. Today, it has a staff of eight and a budget of nearly $1 million.

Heartland operates *PolicyFax*, a fax-on-demand information service featuring research from over one hundred think tanks and advocacy groups. It also publishes *Intellectual Ammunition*, a bimonthly magazine, as well as books, policy studies, and commentaries.

Heartland is a genuinely independent source of research and commentary. It is not affiliated with any political party, business, or foundation. It does not accept government funds and does not conduct "contract" research for special interest groups. Its activities are tax-exempt under Section 501(c)(3) of the Internal Revenue Code.

In 1994, Heartland received the prestigious SPN Roe Award for outstanding leadership on state public policy, and in 1996 it received the Sir Antony Fisher International Memorial Award for its book *Eco-Sanity: A Common-Sense Guide to Environmentalism.*

For more information, visit The Heartland Institute's site on the World Wide Web (http://www.heartland.org), call 847-202-3060, or write to The Heartland Institute, 800 East Northwest Highway #1080, Palatine, IL 60067.

The opinions expressed in this book are those of the author alone. Nothing here should be construed as reflecting the views of The Heartland Institute or as an attempt to aid or hinder the passage of any legislation.

ABOUT THE HEARTLAND INSTITUTE

Board of Directors

Joseph L. Bast	Roy E. Marden
Robert Buford	David H. Padden
Ronald Docksai	Frank Resnik
Theodore Eck	Leslie Rose
Dan Hales	Al St. Clair
John Hosemann	Herbert J. Walberg
James L. Johnston	Lee H. Walker

Staff

Diane Carol Bast	Lisa Doering
Joseph L. Bast	Douglas Kinney
George Clowes	Matthew Nutting
Michael Dixon	Cheryl Parker

167

Board of Policy Advisors

Robert A. Baade
Dean V. Baim
Robert Baird
Michael J. Bakalis
Gordon B. Baldwin
Randy E. Barnett
John H. Beck
Joe A. Bell
Diann G. Benesh
James Bills
Cecil Bohanon
Charles Breeden
Dennis Brennen
Yale Brozen
George Clowes
John L. Conant
Roy Cordato
Douglas J. Den Uyl
Richard M. Ebeling
James D. Fair
David I. Fand
Lowell E. Gallaway
Robert J. Genetski
Gene Grabowski
Donald Haider
Peter J. Hill
J. David Hoeveler Jr.
Steven Horwitz
Harold Hotelling

Lester Hunt
William J. Hunter
Harry Hutchison
Thomas R. Ireland
William B. Irvine
James M. Johannes
James L. Johnston
Nyle B. Kardatzke
Barry Keating
Richard H. Keehn
Bob T. Kleiman
Ross C. Korves
Nicholas A. Lash
George P. Lephardt
Noreen Lephardt
David F. Linowes
David L. Littmann
Yuri N. Maltsev
John McAdams
Robert A. McGuire
Dennis D. Miller
Roman L. Millett
Edwin S. Mills
Gerald Musgrave
Dale Nance
Michael A. Nelson
David Olson
Mack Ott
John B. Parrish

Daniel A. Pavsek
William S. Peirce
Sam Peltzman
Daniel D. Polsby
James D. Regan
Stephen Robinson
Ronald D. Rotunda
Mary J. Ruwart
Lynn Scarlett
Neil Seitz
Parth J. Shah
A. Ross Shepherd
John E. Silvia
John W. Skorburg
W. Gene Smiley
David Sowerby
Douglas Stewart
Thomas S. Ulen
T. Norman Van Cott
Charles Van Eaton
Rickard K. Vedder
Herbert J. Walberg
Thomas F. Walton
Robert Weissberg
Bill Wilson
Tom Wyrick
James V. Young
Philip Zazove